WHAT
NEXT ?

A PRIMER ON PROPHECY

R. E. Harlow

EVERYDAY PUBLICATIONS
TORONTO 13, CANADA

International Standard Book Number: 0-919586-15-5

Printed in Canada

A PRIMER ON PROPHECY

WHAT NEXT?

A PRIMER ON PROPHECY

There are twelve lessons in this book and every lesson contains many paragraphs. Each paragraph has a number; a paragraph with a number is called a Frame. There are over 600 Frames in this book.

You do not have to read all these Frames. Each Frame will tell you which one to read next. In an ordinary book you read right down the page, one paragraph after another. This book is different. You read the next Frame number given; it may be back a page or two, or it may be further ahead. This is how you do it:

Read Frame 01 and the Bible verse given there. At the end of Frame 01 you will see a question with three statements; only one of these statements is true. You should read these three statements and pick out the one which is true.

After each statement you will see the number of the Frame you should go to next. This Frame will tell you if you have the right answer. If you have, you can go on to the next Frame number given. If your answer was wrong, the Frame will tell you where you made a mistake and also tell you what to read next, so you will understand the question better. Then you can read the statements again and pick out the right one.

Here is an example:

Frame 01   God loves everybody in the world, but many people will not believe this. God wanted to prove to all men that He really loves them. He decided to give them a very great Gift. God loved His Son very much but He decided to give His Son so that men can be saved. Now anyone who believes in Christ is saved and has eternal life, John 3.16.

What can we learn from John 3:16? Read the three statements and pick out the right answer; then read the Frame number given.

1.   God loves men, but He hates sin.   FRAME 03

2.   God gave His Son to prove that He loves men and those who believe will receive eternal life right now.

FRAME 04

3.   God loves all men and He will save everybody at last.

FRAME 02

Frame 02   No, this is not true. God does love all men, but He gives eternal life **only** to those who believe in His Son. Read Frame 01 again, also John 3.16, then look for the right answer, 1 or 2.

Frame 03   True, the Bible teaches that God hates sin, but this verse, John 3.16, does not say so. Read the verse again and find the right answer after Frame 01.

Frame 04   Yes, your answer is correct. Now go on to Lesson 1 and Frame 1.

1

THE LORD JESUS

PROMISED TO RETURN

Frame 1 The Lord Jesus had friends. Many people hated Him, but some loved Him. Those who hated Him tried many times to kill Him and at last they succeeded. His friends stayed with Him almost to the end.

On the last night before He died the Lord Jesus talked to His friends and told them what was going to happen. This proved that they were His friends and not just His servants, John 15.15. A master always tells his servants what **they** are going to do, but he does not have to tell them what **he** is going to do. The Lord Jesus told His followers what His Father wanted Him to do.

Which of these three statements is true? Pick out your answer, then go to the Frame number given.

1. The Lord Jesus told His friends what He was going to do. Go to FRAME 4.

2. The Lord Jesus had many enemies, and they found out His secret plans. Go to FRAME 2.

3. A master must tell his servants what he is going to do if he wants them to obey. Go to FRAME 3.

Frame 2 This is not the correct answer. It is true that the Lord had many enemies, but only His friends learned what He was going to do. Read Frame 1 again and pick out the right answer.

Frame 3 No, a master must tell his servants what **they** are going to do. Read John 15.15 and pick out the right answer for Frame 1.

Frame 4 This is true. But how do you become a friend of God? Perhaps you are afraid of God because you do not know how much He loves you. God sent His Son to change us from enemies into His friends, 2 Corinthians 5.18. Believe this good news and you will become a friend of God. Now go on to FRAME 5.

Frame 5 The Lord Jesus told His friends many things that would happen later. One wonderful thing is in John 14.3, *I will come again*. He was going away to prepare a place for them and He promised to come again. He wanted them to be with Him. Where is the Lord Jesus today? He is in heaven and He wants us to be in heaven with Him. We cannot find the way to heaven or get there by ourselves, so He promised to come back again. This is the first great truth we must learn: **the Lord Jesus promised to come back again.**

Which of these three statements is true? Pick out your answer, then go on and read the Frame number given.

1.   Very holy people can get to heaven by themselves.

FRAME 6

2.   The Lord Jesus promised many years ago that He would come back for His friends, but He has never come, so we must understand that He has changed His mind.

FRAME 8

3.   We can be sure the Lord Jesus will come back to earth because He promised to do so.   FRAME 9

Frame 6 No one can find his way to heaven unless Christ takes him there. Read Frame 5 again and pick out the right answer.

Frame 7 Why did the Lord Jesus promise to come back again? One reason is because He loves us and wants us to be with Him. Another thing, God chose the nation of Israel and promised them that He would send a King who will rule for ever. There are many promises like that in the Old Testament. We will study them in Lesson 8, but here we see that Christ must come back because God promised that He will rule as King in this world, Jeremiah 23.5,6. Christ will rule when He comes again.

Think of these three statements and choose the one which gives in short form what is taught in Frame 7. Then read the Frame number given.

1. Christ must come back because it is impossible for God to break His promise.   FRAME 10

2. God's promises in the Old Testament were fulfilled when Christ came the first time.   FRAME 12

3. We cannot force God to keep His promise.   FRAME 11

Frame 8 The Lord Jesus is the Son of God and He will never break His promise. Read the three statements after Frame 5 again and think about your answer.

Frame 9 You are right. Now go to Frame 7.

Frame 10 This statement is the best way to say in short form what Frame 7 teaches. We too should always keep our promises and be faithful to the Lord, but even if we are not faithful, He cannot break His promises or be false to Himself, 2 Timothy 2.13. You are now ready to go on to Frame 13.

11   Of course we cannot **force** God, but we can be sure He will do what He said He would. Read about Abraham in Romans 4.21. Now try again and you will find the right answer to Frame 7.

12   **Some** of God's promises were fulfilled when Christ came the first time, but God also promised He will rule. Read Jeremiah 23.5,6 again, also Isaiah 32.1 and Frame 7, then choose your answer, 1 or 3. ·

13   Here is another reason why God wants Christ to return to this world. God's Son came the first time and did perfectly all that His Father wanted Him to do. God said He was well pleased with His Son, Matthew 3.17; 17.5. Men did not accept the Lord Jesus and God allowed them to beat Him and spit on Him and kill Him. Then God raised Him from death and put Him on His own throne in heaven, Acts 5.30,31; Hebrews 8.1. Today all who are in heaven give honour to Christ, but it is necessary that people on earth should do the same. God will never be satisfied until all men know that He has chosen and accepted Christ.

Think of the following statements and decide which one is correct. Then go on to the Frame number given.

1. God has given great glory to His Son in heaven, so it is not necessary for Christ to return to earth.   FRAME 16

2. Men reject the Son of God, but God wants all men to honour Him on earth as well as in heaven.   FRAME 14

3. Men killed the Lord Jesus when He came the first time and God will not let Him return to the earth because men would want to kill Him again.   FRAME 18

14   Yes, this is the main point in Frame 13. Now you may go on to Frame 15.

15   Long ago God had promised that He would send His Son to rule as King in this world. God promised Adam and Eve that their Seed or Descendant would get the victory over Satan, even though Satan had led them to commit sin, Genesis 3.15. He promised Abraham that all nations would be blessed through his Descendant, Genesis 22.18; Galatians 3.16. God was looking forward to the coming of Christ when He promised that David's Son or Descendant will rule for ever, 2 Samuel 7.16. Christ came once, but He did not rule over men. He will come again and fulfill God's promises in the Old Testament, Psalm 2.6,7.

Which of these three statements is true?

1. God promised that Christ would come to rule and He will surely do so.   FRAME 17

2. God promised to do good to men, but men have always disobeyed Him, so He can change His promises and judge men as they deserve.   FRAME 19

3. Christ came to earth and many people believed on Him and accepted Him as their King. So these Old Testament promises have already been fulfilled and there is no need for Christ to return.   FRAME 20

16   The first part of your answer is correct, but still God requires that His Son should have honour on earth. Read

Mark 14.62 and Frame 13 again very carefully, and you will see which answer is correct.

17   You have chosen the correct statement. Now go on to Frame 21.

18   No doubt men would want to kill Christ again, but Frame 13 shows that God requires all men to honour His Son, so Christ will come with great power. Look up 2 Thessalonians 1.7,8 and read Frame 13, then select the correct answer.

19   You are partly right. Some of God's promises depend on man's obedience; these promises begin with the word *if*. But many of God's promises just tell us what God is going to do and do not depend on anyone. God said that Christ will rule in this world and so He will. Think of the statements after Frame 15 again and pick out the right one.

20   It is true that many people accepted Christ as Lord and many are doing so today, but this is not the same as ruling over the world. Read Psalm 72.11 and read Frame 15 again. Then pick out the right answer.

21   We have seen some very good reasons to believe that Christ will come again. (If you are not sure about this go back to Frames 1, 5, 7, 13 and 15 again.) Still some people do not want to believe He is coming again. They try to explain these verses in different ways.

Is any one of the following statements true? Read the Frame number given so you will be able to answer this kind of teaching.

1.   The Holy Spirit is God and He came into the world after Christ died. When the Lord Jesus said, I will come again, He just meant that the Holy Spirit would come.
                                                        FRAME 22

2.   Christ comes into the heart of every man when he believes in Him. This is what it means when it says Christ is coming.
                                                        FRAME 24

3.   The Lord said, "I will come and take you to myself." This means when a believer dies the Lord takes him to heaven.
                                                        FRAME 25

22   The Holy Spirit is indeed God and He came into the world, but He is not a man, He was not nailed to the cross and He is not ruling as King on David's throne. The Holy Spirit Himself said many times in the New Testament that Christ **will** come again. We will study 1 Thessalonians 4.16 in the next lesson. In many other verses in this book the Holy Spirit tells us that the Lord Himself will come. If you understand this Frame, go to Frame 21 again and read statement 2.

23   Many people teach these things and perhaps you think this is what the Bible means, but the Bible really teaches that the Lord **Himself** will come just as He went away. Read Frame 26 again and remember that Christ will come suddenly and with clouds, Mark 13.26; Matthew 26.64. Now read sentences 2 and 3 after Frame 26 and decide which is correct.

24   This is partly true; Christ comes into our hearts when we receive Him as our Saviour, John 1.12, but this does not fulfill **all** God's promises. Christ rules in our hearts, but He certainly is not ruling in this world today. This is **not** what the Bible means when we read He is coming again. Now look at statement 3 at the end of Frame 21.

25   Does John 14.3 mean that Christ comes to take us to heaven when we die? It could mean that, but we know from other verses that the Lord is really coming back into this world. It is important to learn that no verse in the Bible can be taken by itself. You must try to understand **all** the verses which speak about the same subject. Now go on to Frame 26.

26   You see that Christ Himself must come back to fulfill God's promises and His own promises. After Jesus arose from death He talked with His disciples and taught them many things. They saw Him, heard Him speak, ate with Him, touched His body. One day He was speaking to them on the Mount of Olives and as they watched Him He was taken up into a cloud. Two angels came and told them that this Jesus was taken up into heaven, and He will come back in the same way that they saw Him go into heaven, Acts 1.11. *This Jesus will come in the same way.*

Which of these statements is correct?

1. We should teach people to do good and to love one another, and then Christ will come into their hearts. Finally all men will believe in God, and the Kingdom of God will come.   FRAME 23

2. The angels' words in Acts 1.11 prove that the Lord Himself will come in a cloud and people will see Him, the Man Christ Jesus.   FRAME 27

3. Christ is on His Father's throne and He will never leave it again. He will send an angel to take the Church to heaven.   FRAME 29

27   This is the only correct statement. Go to Frame 30.

28   This is true. If you understand these points go on to Frame 32.

29   Christ is at the Father's right hand and will stay there until the time comes. Read Psalm 110.1 and notice the word *until.* Read 1 Thessalonians 4.16 and notice the word *Himself.* Then go back to Frame 26 and pick out the true statement.

30   The Lord Jesus not only promised to come back to earth, but He promised to come quickly or soon, Revelation 22.7, 12,20. It is now about 1,900 years since He made that promise. Some people get tired of waiting and fall into worldly sin, like the servant in Luke 12.45. Others say there must be some mistake and they try to explain the Lord's promises by saying He meant something else. But we should remember three things:

1. The Lord Jesus wants us to be with Him more than we want to go to heaven. Why then does He not come quickly?

2. When Christ comes the day of God's grace will be over. God would like all men to turn from their sins and be saved, 2 Peter 3.9.

3. It seems like a long time to us, but a thousand years is like one day only for God, 2 Peter 3.8. When the right time comes the Lord will return and when He returns He will come soon or quickly.

Which of these three statements is correct?

1. The Lord said He would come quickly; this means He will come at once when the day of grace is over and the Father's time arrives.   FRAME 28

2. It is 1,900 years since the New Testament was written and nothing has happened. Some people still think that Christ will come again, but this is silly.   FRAME 31

3. The Lord Jesus really thought that He would soon return but He has to wait until the Father sends Him back.
                                                                FRAME 33

31   God knew long ago that men would laugh at Christ's promise to return. The Holy Spirit told Peter that this would happen in the last days, 2 Peter 3.3,4. Many people today make fun of Christians who believe that Christ is coming back. This proves that we are in the last days and the Lord will come soon. Read again the verses which are given in Frame 30. Then find the correct statement, 1 or 3.

32   The Lord Jesus promised to come back and to come quickly. Before He went away He also promised to send the Holy Spirit, John 16.7.

```
If I go – I will send the Comforter   John 16.7
If I go – I will come again           John 14.3
```

The Holy Spirit came to teach us all things and to show us things to come, John 14.26; 16.13. The teaching of the Holy Spirit is in the Bible and He has told us many things which are still in the future. In this book we will look at some of the great chapters of the Bible which tell us about coming events:

1 Thessalonians 4 tells how Christ will come for His Church.

Daniel 2 tells about four great kingdoms.

Daniel 7 and 8 tell more about the kingdoms, especially the fourth one in the last days.

Matthew 24 tells what will happen before the Lord comes.

Revelation 2 and 3 tell about the Church at the present time.

Revelation 19-21 tell us about many things which will happen after Christ comes.

2 Thessalonians 2 shows us the Man of Sin.

Revelation 13 tells about the beast and the False Prophet.

Revelation 6-16 tell us about the Great Tribulation.

Revelation 17 and 18 show us Babylon, the great prostitute.

We will study these chapters a little at a time and many other verses as well. Let us ask God to help us to understand His wonderful plans as He has revealed them in the Bible.

When the Lord Jesus went back to heaven the Holy Spirit came down from heaven. What is the most important work of the Holy Spirit? His greatest work is to give glory to the Lord Jesus. He has told us many things about the future, and, best of all, that Christ will come in glory. You will learn what will happen next in God's plan, but the most important thing is to love Christ more. Now go on to Frame 34.

33   Your answer might be the words of a person who thinks that the Lord may have made a mistake or said something which is not true. The Lord always spoke the words which His Father gave Him, John 8.28. Read Frame 30 again and look up all the verses. Then pick out the right answer, 1 or 2.

Chart 1

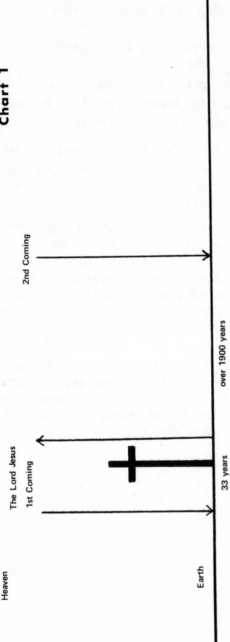

Heaven

The Lord Jesus
1st Coming

2nd Coming

Earth

33 years

over 1900 years

34   Look at Chart 1 and find first the cross in the middle of the line. This cross stands for the time when the Lord Jesus died. Before He died He came down from heaven and after He died He went back to heaven, John 16.28. Now He is in heaven, but He is coming back again.

The Lord Jesus was about 33 years old when He died, so there were 33 years between the time He came from the Father and the time He went back to the Father. We do not know just when the Lord will come again, but already 1,900 years have passed since the time He went up to heaven. Go to Frame 35 in Lesson 2.

THE RAPTURE

35 We have seen that the Lord promised to return, but first He sent the Holy Spirit to lead us into all truth, John 16.13. The Holy Spirit did lead men to write the 27 books of the New Testament. About half of these were written by one man, the apostle Paul. In this chapter we will look at two letters written by Paul. We can be sure the Holy Spirit led Paul to write the truth.

Read the first letter to the Thessalonians, chapter 4, verses 13-18. What do these verses teach us? Pick out the right answer and then go on to the next Frame number.

1. These verses teach that we should not be sad about Christians who die before the Lord comes. FRAME 36

2. When the Lord comes He will take all living Christians to heaven, but those who have died will not go until later. FRAME 38

3. The Lord will come from heaven, Christians who died will rise from death and those who are alive will be caught up to meet the Lord. FRAME 40

36 The first verse, verse 13, teaches that we should not be sad in the same way as those who do not know God. But there is much more teaching in verses 13-18. Read these six verses again and try to see what are the most important things. Then read answers 2 and 3 and pick out the right one.

37 You have chosen the correct answer. Go to Frame 42.

38 Read verses 16 and 17 very carefully and you will see what will happen first and what comes next. Then try again to find the right answer.

39   Now look at verse 13. Some of the Christians were very sad because a few of the believers had died. The Christians in Thessalonica had many enemies, Acts 17.5, and perhaps some believers had been killed. Paul was with the Thessalonians only three weeks, but he taught them about the Lord's return, 1 Thessalonians 1.10; 2 Thessalonians 2.5. They believed this and when their friends died it made them very sad. Paul said they should not be like those who do not believe in God.

Which of these statements is true?

1.   When a believer dies we should not mourn and be sad like other people because we have a real hope that the Lord will come.   FRAME 37

2.   The Christians in Thessalonica were afraid because their enemies had killed some of them and would soon attack others.   FRAME 41

3.   The believers were sad because they did not know the wonderful truth that Christ will return.   FRAME 44

40   This statement gives in short form the main teaching of these verses. Now go to Frame 39 and we will look at these words more carefully.

41   Maybe they were afraid that more of them would get killed, but verse 13 does not say so. Read this verse again, also Frame 39, then look for the correct answer.

42   Every true Christian believes that the Lord Jesus died and rose again. We should also believe that He will come back to the world and bring with Him those believers who have died, verse 14. Some Bibles say these believers are "asleep in Jesus". The word *sleep* is used for a believer who has died. For example, the Lord said Lazarus was sleeping, but He meant that he had died, John 11.11,13. This word *sleep* means that a believer is not dead forever, but his body is resting until the Lord comes. It does not mean that he is unconscious or cannot think. Paul taught that we will be very happy the minute we die because our spirits will be with Christ, Philippians 1.23. Here Paul says that Christ will bring with Him all believers who have died.

Which of these is correct?

1.   The Lord will bring with Him all believers who died before He comes.   FRAME 43

2.   A person can believe in Christ and not believe that He will come again.   FRAME 45

3.   When you die, that is the end of everything. FRAME 47

4.   Every Christian will die and will rise again from death, but until Christ comes he is like a person who is asleep, he cannot feel or think about anything.   FRAME 48

43   This is true. Turn to Frame 46.

44   Christians may indeed be sad if they do not know about the Lord's coming, but Paul had taught the Thessalonian Christians this great truth. Read 1 Thessalonians 1.10; 2 Thessalonians 2.5, then read Frame 39 again and find the right answer.

45   It is true that some Christians do not believe that the Lord will come again, but Christ is the Son of God and cannot lie. All who believe in Christ should believe His promise to come again. However many Christians have never been taught these wonderful truths. Read the first part of Frame 42 again and look for the right answer.

46   Paul said he was teaching these things because the Lord had taught him, v.15. The Lord Jesus had promised to send the Holy Spirit and He would show us things which will happen in the future. Even the apostles did not know these truths until Paul wrote this chapter.

   The first thing we learn is that we who are alive will not go to heaven before those believers who have already died. We see at once that God knows all future events and He knows the order of these events. He knows what will happen first, what will happen next and what will happen last. God has all power and controls everything completely. He has told us these things because He loves us.

Pick out the true statement:

1.   Men have always looked forward to a wonderful time on earth in the future and here Paul was full of the same idea.
                                                        FRAME 49
2.   God the Holy Spirit showed Paul future events and the order of those events. God knows all and controls all.
                                                        FRAME 50
3.   Satan is very active today and all true believers will be killed before the Lord comes again, but Christ will raise them from death.   FRAME 53

47   Many men teach this, but the Bible certainly does not. These verses plainly show that believers will live again and other verses teach that all men will live again, John 5.28-29. Read Frame 42 again and choose the right answer.

48   No; the Christian will be very happy when he dies because he will be with the Lord. Read Philippians 1.23 very carefully. To be with Christ is far better than to fall asleep and not be able to feel or think about anything. Read Frame 42 again, and try to find the right answer.

49   Paul was not teaching the Thessalonians what everybody was hoping for. Paul received a special revelation from God, the Holy Spirit. Read the first part of verse 15, and the first part of Frame 46, then think carefully about statements 2 and 3.

50   This statement is true. You are ready to go to Frame 51.

51   The Lord Jesus went up to heaven and He **Himself** will come down again. There will be three sounds: we will hear a shout, the voice of an angel, and the sound of God's trumpet, v.16. The Lord Jesus will command His people to rise up and meet Him. Michael is called the archangel in Jude 9; he was one of the chief princes who fought for Israel, Daniel 10.13,21; 12.1; Revelation 12.7.

   In Israel someone would blow the trumpet to call the people together and command them to move forward, Numbers 10.3,5,6.

We can be very sure that every true believer will hear the command of the Lord when He comes for us.

Which of these statements is true?

1. The Lord Jesus will come for His people and all of us will hear His voice when He commands us to rise up and meet Him.   FRAME 52

2. Some Christians love this world and they will not hear the Lord's voice when He calls.   FRAME 54

3. Christ will call the Christians and the archangel will call the Jews to rise from death.   FRAME 56

52 Yes, this is true. Go to Frame 55.

53 Satan is very active today and he would like to kill us all, but there will certainly be many believers still alive when Jesus comes. Verses 15 and 17 speak of living believers here on earth when the great day arrives. Go back to Frame 46 and find the true statement.

54 Many Christians do love the world, but true believers are like sheep who know the Shepherd's voice, John 10.27. The Lord Jesus will be able to make them hear and obey. Read the last sentence in Frame 51 again, then read the first and third statements and pick out the right one.

55 We have seen in Frame 46 that God knows all future events and knows the order in which they will happen. Now read 1 Thessalonians 4.16,17.

Which of these three events will come first?

1. Christians who have died will be raised from death.
                                                                          FRAME 59

2. The Lord comes down with a shout.   FRAME 58

3. Living Christians will be gathered to meet the Lord in the air.   FRAME 60

56 The archangel will indeed speak when Christ comes and Michael is the angel who helps Israel, but when the Lord returns we will all be together with Him forever. Read 1 Thessalonians 4.16, also Frame 51 again, then select the right answer.

57   It is hard to understand how our bodies could go up to a cloud in the air, but remember that God has all power: He can raise people from death, He can raise them to the cloud. He would not raise the bodies of believers from death if only their spirits were to go to heaven; in fact the spirits are in heaven now, with the Lord. Read 2 Corinthians 5.8 and then study answers 2 and 3 after Frame 61.

58   Yes, this is the first thing to happen. We will hear His shout when He comes. Dead Christians will rise before we do and we will all meet the Lord in the air. Read more about this in Frame 61.

59   Dead Christians will be raised *first:* this means before the living Christians are caught up. But the first thing is, the Lord will come. The correct order is the way Paul put it in 1 Thessalonians 4.16 and 17. Read Frame 58.

60   No, the statement you have chosen (living Christians will be gathered to meet the Lord) really is the last of these events, but all will take place very quickly. First Christ will come for us and call us to be with Himself. Read Frame 58.

61   It is good to know that dead Christians will rise from death when the Lord comes for all His people. We who are alive will hear the shout and will be caught up with them. The Spirit of God caught Philip away when his work in the desert was finished, Acts 8.39. And God's power is great enough to take up all believers at the same time. We will be caught up:

> with all other believers,
> in the clouds,
> to meet the Lord,
> in the air, 1 Thessalonians 4.16,17

This great event is called the **Rapture** because we will be caught up by God's power. It is also sometimes called the **translation** because we will be changed, as Enoch was, Hebrews 11.5. We will learn more about being changed in Frame 74, but in this book we will use the word **Rapture**.

What is the **Rapture**? Pick out the right answer and go to the Frame number given.

1. The Rapture means that the spirits of all believers will go to heaven.   FRAME 57

2. The Rapture means that all believers, body, soul and spirit, will meet the Lord in the air.   FRAME 62

3. The Rapture will be like Philip's: when each man's work is done he will be taken away.   FRAME 65

62   Yes, dead believers will first rise from death and their spirits will enter their bodies again. We who are still alive will go with them to meet the Lord. Go on to Frame 63.

63   What happens next after we meet the Lord in the air? **We will be with the Lord forever.** This was His desire, John 12.26; 14.3; and in John 17.24 He prayed that we should be with Him. Christ will be happy to have us with Him and we will be happy to be with Him. We will see Him and we will be like Him, 1 John 3.2. We will go wherever He goes. When He is in heaven we will be in heaven. When He comes to earth, we will come to earth. We will be with Him forever.

What does *forever* mean?

1. God will live forever and will never have an end. We will be with Christ as long as God lives.   FRAME 64

2. If we fall into sin in heaven God will change His mind and put us out.   FRAME 66

3. After thousands of years everyone will become part of God and we will no longer exist as separate persons.
                                                                        FRAME 69

64   This is correct and it is wonderful to know this truth. Now go to Frame 67.

65   No, these verses teach that we will all go together. When Christians die they go to heaven one by one. The Rapture means that many believers will not die; they will be caught up alive into the air and then go to heaven. Read 1 Thessalonians 4.16,17 and read Frame 61 again, then look for the real meaning of the Rapture.

66   There will be no sin in heaven and we will never sin there. We will see the Lord and be like Him and of course He cannot sin. We will be with Christ forever. Read the answers after Frame 63 again and pick out the right one.

67   So here in 1 Thessalonians 4 we have this wonderful promise that the Lord Jesus Christ will come for His people and we will be with Him forever. What effect should this promise have on us today? Perhaps we are having a lot of trouble or the men of the world hate us and hurt us. Cheer up! The Lord is coming soon, 1 Thessalonians 4.18... Some other believers are getting careless and becoming too friendly with the people of this world. This is because they refuse to obey God in their hearts, Romans 12.2. They need to be warned and to keep themselves pure, 1 John 3.3... Other Christians love the Lord and are trying to serve Him. They should try to help those who are in trouble and teach them that the Lord is coming back soon... Think about these things, then go to Frame 68.

68   We have seen some wonderful things in 1 Thessalonians 4; now let us turn to another great chapter, 1 Corinthians 15, and read verses 51-54.

What is the *main* teaching of these verses?

1.   Paul told the Corinthians the secret mystery which he knew.   FRAME 70
2.   These verses tell us that we will have victory over death.   FRAME 72
3.   Our bodies will be changed when the Lord comes.
                                    FRAME 73

69   The priests of Buddha teach this but the Bible certainly does not. We will be men, like Christ, and with Him forever. Read Frame 63 again and find the right answer.

70   Paul did tell the Corinthians a secret or a mystery, but this is not the **main** teaching of verses 51-54. What is this mystery about? Read these verses again very carefully and find the right answer, 2 or 3.

71   Not slowly but suddenly. We will be changed in a second. Read verses 51 and 52 again and look for the right answer.

72   This is true, we will have victory over death, but what is the most important thing which Paul taught in verses 51-54? Read these verses again and try to find the right answer, 1 or 3.

73   Yes, this is correct. Paul said twice that we will be changed, at the end of verse 51 and at the end of verse 52. Then he explained the great changes which will take place, vs.53,54. Go on to Frame 74.

74   Let us now look more carefully at these verses in 1 Corinthians 15.51-54. We see that we will be suddenly changed when the Lord comes, vs.51,52. This change will take place in a second, in the time it takes to blink your eye. One minute we will still be ordinary men who could be killed at any time and the next minute we will have bodies which can never die. This great change will take place when we hear the last trumpet and the Lord comes.

Which of these four statements is true?

1.   We will slowly become more like the Lord when we get to heaven.   FRAME 71

2.   When Christ comes our bodies will die and we will get new bodies.   FRAME 75

3.   Our bodies will be changed and we will never have to die.
                                                        FRAME 77

4.   We will put on the new body which cannot die, but we will also have the old body which we have right now.
                                                        FRAME 79

75   No, we will not all die, v.51; Frame 42. Look again at the
four answers after Frame 74 and pick out the right one.

76   Men have tried to tell when the Lord will come, but the
Lord Jesus said that no man can know just when it will be.
Read Matthew 24.36 and read Frame 80 again, then select the
right answer.

77   You are right and this is the only right answer for Frame 74,
Before you go on, read 1 Corinthians 15.58. Here God
tells us to stand firm and keep busy in our work for the Lord.
Then He promises that anything we do for Him will always be
valuable. We will soon see in Frame 87 that He will give rich
rewards to those who serve Him. But first go to Frame 78.

78   These bodies will be changed when the Lord comes. We
have read about God's trumpet in 1 Thessalonians 4.16
and Frame 51; the Holy Spirit spoke of the *last* trumpet in 1 Corinthians 15.52. We also noted that dead believers will rise first,
before we are changed and caught up to the air. If you are not
sure about these things you can go back to 1 Thessalonians 4.16,17
and also read Frame 55 again. In 1 Corinthians 15 we also learn
that death itself will be destroyed, see verses 26 and 54.

We have carefully studied parts of two great chapters which
tell us about the Rapture. Some important truths are found in
1 Thessalonians 4.13-18; others are in 1 Corinthians 15.51-54;
some are in both. You should know where these truths are found
so you can teach other Christians about the Lord's return. In the
list below you can test yourself by showing where these things are
taught. Look up the verses in the Bible if you are not sure.

Put T or C or TC or O or X after each statement, 1 to 15.
T means: this is in 1 Thessalonians 4.13-18.
C means: this is in 1 Corinthians 15.51-54.
TC means: this is in both chapters.
O means: that this is true, but is not found in either of
these chapters.
X means: this is not true.

1. The Lord will come from heaven. ....
2. The Lord wants us to be with Him. ....
3. The shout. ....
4. The voice of Michael. ....
5. The trumpet will sound. ....
6. Some true Christians love this world and will not hear the Lord's voice when He calls us. ....
7. The dead Christians will rise. ....
8. We will all be changed in a second. ....
9. We will put on a body which cannot die. ....
10. The living Christians will be caught up. ....
11. We will meet the Lord in the air. ....
12. We will see Him and be like Him. ....
13. Only our spirits will go to heaven. ....
14. Victory over death. ....
15. When you die that is the end of everything. ....

When you have written down your answers go next to Frame 81.

79   From verses 53 and 54, you might think that we just put on a better body and also keep the old one, but this is not so. Every man has only one body. When Christ comes we will put off the weaknesses of this body and we will never have to die. Read Frame 74 again and find the right answer.

80   The Rapture will be a wonderful time for the Lord Jesus and for all believers. When will it be? When will the Lord come? We do not know exactly when the Lord will come, but we believe it will be soon.

The Lord Jesus Himself said He did not know the day nor the hour when He will come. No man knew when the Lord would come, the angels did not know, only the Father knows, Mark 13.32. Later the Lord told His disciples that the Father keeps control of the future, Acts 1.7. However, God has told us many things which will happen in the future after the Rapture, and we believe He is now preparing the world for these things. In Lesson 11 we will study a little of what is going on in the world, things which show that the coming of the Lord is near. Some people have tried to set dates when the Lord will return, but nothing happened. We should wait with patience until the Father's time comes.

Which of these statements is true?

1. Men can study the book of Daniel and the pyramids of Egypt and tell the year when the Lord will come.

    FRAME 76

2. It is almost 2,000 years since the Lord promised to return and it could be another thousand before He comes.

    FRAME 82

3. Only God knows just when the Lord will return, but we think it will be soon.   FRAME 85

81   You should have written T after statements 1, 3, 4, 10, 11 because these truths are found in 1 Thessalonians 4.13-18, but not in 1 Corinthians 15.

You should have written C after statements 8, 9, 14, because they are in 1 Corinthians 15, not in 1 Thessalonians 4.

You should have written TC after statements 5 and 7 because they are in both chapters.

You should have written 0 after statements 2 and 12 because they are true and are found in the Bible, but not in 1 Thessalonians 4 or 1 Corinthians 15.

You should have written X after statements 6, 13 and 15 because they are not true.

If you understand this Frame, go to Frame 80.

82   We do not know when the Lord will come, but there are many things today which seem to show that He will come soon. Read the last part of Frame 80 again. Then look for the right answer.

83   Good, this is correct. Go to Frame 87.

84   All believers will be very happy when the Lord comes, but some will be happier than others. The Bible tells us that a very serious event will take place soon after the Rapture. This is called the Judgment Seat of Christ, Romans 14.10-12; 2 Corinthians 5.8-10. We must all stand before the Son of God to be judged by Him. Many Christians work very hard to please the Lord and serve Him well; they will receive great rewards. Other true Christians live in sin and are friendly with the world. They will lose their rewards but not their eternal life, 1 Corinthians 3.15. When the Lord comes, only true believers will go to heaven and stand before Him at the Judgment Seat of Christ. People who do not believe will be judged at the Great White Throne. We will read about this in Lesson 7.

Which of these statements is true?

1. All believers will stand before the Judgment Seat of Christ and those who have served the Lord will get rewards.   FRAME 83

2. If I have done more good things than bad, God will let me go to heaven.   FRAME 86

3. All men must bow before the Lord at the Judgment Seat of Christ.   FRAME 89

85   This is true. Now read Frame 84.

86   Many people suppose that God will forgive our sins if we do enough good things, but this is certainly not true. One sin makes you a sinner and God will forgive you only if you believe in Christ. Read Titus 3.5 and study Frame 84 again so you will be able to pick the right answer.

87   What will happen at the Judgment Seat of Christ? The Bible speaks of *crowns* and *rewards*. Some will receive a crown of righteousness, 2 Timothy 4.8; others, a crown of glory, 1 Peter 5.4. The Lord Jesus knows all about us; He knows those who have served Him well. Some believers will stand before the Lord and hear Him say, "Well done, good and faithful servant," Matthew 25.21,23. These believers will have great joy when they hear these things. Of course the Lord will not speak these words unless they are true. Many Christians waste their time and do nothing for the Lord. They will be saved, but will have no reward, 1 Corinthians 3.15.

Choose the one true statement:

1. At the Judgment Seat of Christ some believers will receive crowns, and some will get rewards, but some will not receive anything.   FRAME 88

2. Those believers who have not served the Lord will be put out of heaven.   FRAME 90

3. The Lord loves everyone and will tell us all that we were good and faithful servants.   FRAME 95

88   You are right. This is the only time to earn these rewards or crowns. It will soon be too late. You should give yourself to the Lord right now and ask Him how you can serve Him best. Now go on to Frame 92.

89   All men must bow before Christ, Philippians 2.10, but wicked men will be judged about a thousand years after the Judgment Seat of Christ. Read again the last part of Frame 84 and look for the right answer.

90   No, this is not true. We are not saved because of our good works and God does not put us out of heaven because we failed. However He will give rewards only to those who have served Him well. One man in Matthew 25.30 was thrown out but he did not really know the Lord, v.24. Read Titus 3.5 and Frame 87 again and look for the right answer.

91   This is correct. Now you understand the Chart and the teaching of Lesson 2. You may go on to Lesson 3 and Frame 97.

92   Think of God's wonderful love to us! He saves sinners just because we believe in Christ. Good works are not necessary to take us to heaven. But if we do serve Him He gives us the strength we need **and** He will give us great rewards in heaven, rewards which we will have forever. Stop here and thank the Lord in your heart for all His love to you.

     No answer is required for Frame 92. You may now go to Frame 96.

93   Three of the four arrows show the direction Christ went or will go, but one arrow speaks of the Church. Read the second part of Frame 96 and try again.

94   Your answer is true but the question is, What do these arrows **mean**? Read the second part of Frame 96 again and find the correct answer.

95   The Lord loves us and will not put us out of heaven, but He will never say what is not true. He will give rewards to many believers, but not to all. Some people will be happier than others when we get to heaven. Read 1 Corinthians 3.13-15, then look again for the right answer.

96   Now look at Chart 2. In Frame 34 (last part) we noticed that the cross tells about the time when the Son of God died for our sins. Before that He came down from heaven; and after He died He went back to His Father. He promised to return, but first the Good News is to go out to every nation. The Church Age comes between the time when Christ went to heaven and the day He will come back.

On Chart 1 an arrow pointed **down** to show that Christ will return as He promised. But in Lesson 2 we learned that the Lord will first come to the cloud to meet us in the air. So in Chart 2 one arrow shows Christ coming down and another shows the Church going up to meet Him. Then after this the Lord will examine each believer at the Judgment Seat of Christ.

Chart 2

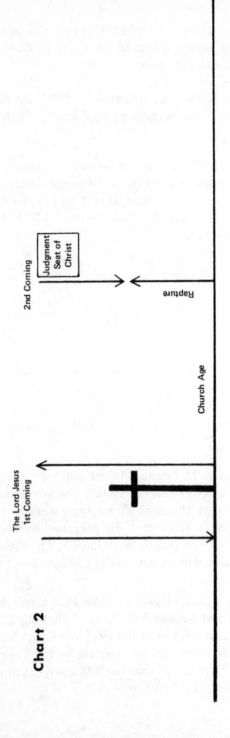

The Lord Jesus
1st Coming

Church Age

2nd Coming

Judgment
Seat of
Christ

Rapture

Do you understand Chart 2? What do the four arrows mean?

1. Two arrows point down and two point up.   FRAME 94

2. Christ came down to earth, then went up to heaven. He will come back almost to the world and all believers will be caught up to meet Him in the air.   FRAME 91

3. The arrows show the way that Christ went, both up and down.   FRAME 93

THE KING'S

3

DREAM

97   We have seen some of the Lord's promises in the New
Testament and there are many more in the Old Testament.
There were 16 men of God called *prophets,* who wrote the last
17 books in the Old Testament, Isaiah to Malachi. First we will
read in the book of Daniel the prophet. Some people say today
that Daniel was just a great writer who could tell good stories, but
the Lord Jesus Christ called him a *prophet,* Matthew 24.15. We
can be sure that God showed Daniel many things which would
happen in the future. Some of these things have already happened
and others will take place when the Lord comes.

Which of these is true?

1.   Jesus called Daniel a prophet, but He said this because all
the people thought Daniel was a true prophet and Jesus
wanted to please them.   FRAME 99

2.   The Lord Jesus said that Daniel was a prophet and so we
know that his words are true.   FRAME 102

3.   Daniel was a prophet of God and everything he said has
happened just as he told it.   FRAME 105

98   Sometimes people begin to say wonderful things about a
person long after he has died. But Ezekiel lived at the
same time as Daniel and the Holy Spirit showed Ezekiel what to
say about Daniel. Read Ezekiel 14.14,20 again, and the first part
of Frame 100.

99   The Lord Jesus is the Son of God and He knew that God
had spoken through Daniel. The Lord was never afraid to
tell the truth, even if it made the people angry. Read John 10.31,
32, then read Frame 97 again and pick out the right answer.

100   Daniel was known as a very righteous man while he was
        still alive. Ezekiel lived at the same time as Daniel and
Ezekiel put him with Noah and Job as three great and righteous
men, Ezekiel 14.14,20.

Daniel started to serve the Lord while he was a young man.
The king of Babylon took Daniel and his three friends as prisoners
and wanted to teach them to be wise men in Babylon. He gave
them food and wine, but Daniel would not eat or drink. These
things had been offered to the false gods of Babylon and Daniel
wanted to serve Jehovah the God of Israel. His three friends did
the same. God made them very wise and the king of Babylon
found them to be wiser than all other wise men who were much
older. You can read this story in Daniel 1.

Now ask yourself which of these three statements is true.

1.   Long after Daniel died people thought he was a great
      man and called him a prophet.   FRAME 98

2.   Daniel wanted to serve the Lord and God made him very
      wise.   FRAME 103

3.   The king became angry when David refused to eat his
      meat and drink his wine, so the king threw him to the
      lions.   FRAME 106

101   No, they said they would be able to tell him what his
        dream meant if he would tell them what he had dreamed,
v.4. Their gods could not help them. Read Frame 104 again and
look for the right answer.

102   This is true. Now go to Frame 100.

103   This is true. God will tell His secrets only to those who are
        willing to live for Him and obey His commands, Amos 3.7.
You may now go to Frame 104.

104   Daniel was soon able to use all the wisdom God had given
        him. Read Daniel 2.1-23. One night the king of Babylon
had a dream and the next morning he could not remember what
it was. The "wise men" in Babylon were priests or worshippers of
the false gods, and could not tell the king what he had seen in the

dream. Daniel and his three friends asked the God of heaven to show them what the king had dreamed. God answered their prayer and Daniel was able to tell the king what he had dreamed and what the dream meant.

Would you like to understand God's plan for the future? Notice that Daniel loved the Lord and refused to eat food which had been offered to idols. He kept himself separate from the world and we must do the same. Another thing, he prayed for wisdom, and so should we, James 1.5. Then God answered Daniel's prayer and Daniel gave Him the praise, Daniel 2.30. God will not give us wisdom if it will make us proud, 1 Peter 5.6. We must do as Daniel did if we want to know God's plans for the future.

Which of these statements is true?

1. The wise men of Babylon told the king what he had dreamed, but they could not tell him what his dream meant.   FRAME 101

2. Anyone can know God's plans for the future if he will just study the Bible.   FRAME 107

3. To understand God's plans we must be separate from the world, we must ask God to teach us, and not become proud.   FRAME 108

105   Daniel was a true prophet, but many things in his book have not happened **yet**. We can be sure they will happen later. Read the last part of Frame 97 and find the right answer.

106   It was dangerous to refuse the king's meat and wine, but God helped His young servants and the king did not punish them, or throw them to the lions. You are thinking of what happened later in Daniel 6. Read Daniel 1.11-21 and then Frame 100 again. This will help you find the right statement.

107   Many people study the Bible, but they do not really understand God's plans for the future. What should they do? Read the second part of Frame 104 again, then pick out the right answer.

108   This is correct, now go on to Frame 109.

109   What then did the king see in his dream? Read Daniel
2.31-35. The king saw an image like a man, but made of
metal: the head was gold, the arms and part of the body were
silver; the rest of the body and part of the legs were brass; the
lower legs were iron and the feet were partly iron and partly clay.
Suddenly a stone fell on the feet of the image and the whole
thing was broken to pieces. In fact, all these different metals were
ground up as fine as dust and the wind blew it all away. But the
stone became a great mountain which filled the whole earth.

Answer **all three** of these questions:

1.   Which part of the image was the most valuable?

_____

2.   Why were the feet weak? _____

_____

3.   Where did the stone come from? _____

_____

Write in your answers to all three questions, then go to
Frame 114.

110   No, these four kingdoms did not exist at the same time,
but they followed one another. The first was the kingdom
of Babylon and after it another kingdom would become strong,
then another, and another. Read verses 39 and 40 and study
Frame 112 again so you can pick the right answer.

111   True. Now go on to Frame 119.

112   What did King Nebuchadnezzar's dream mean? Read Daniel
2.36-43. Daniel said that the four parts of the image were
like four kingdoms which follow one after another. The gold head
was a picture of the kingdom of Nebuchadnezzar. After him there
would be two more kingdoms which would rule over the whole
world, but they would not have as much glory as the first one.

The fourth kingdom was very strong for a while, like iron which can break anything, but later the iron was mixed with clay, which is not as strong as metal. This kingdom would be divided and part of it would be weak.

What did the king's dream mean? Pick out the right answer.

1. There would be four kingdoms which would fight each other until one got the victory.   FRAME 110

2. The image showed that there would be four kingdoms one after another. The first would be glorious and the last would be weak and divided.   FRAME 113

3. The king's dream meant that there had been four kingdoms, each one more glorious than the one before, and Nebuchadnezzar was the gold head.   FRAME 116

113   Yes, this statement gives in short form the meaning of Nebuchadnezzar's dream. Now go on to Frame 117.

114   1. The head was made of *gold* which was the most valuable metal in the image.

2. The legs were made of iron which is very strong, but the feet were *mixed with clay,* so they were weak. When the stone hit the feet the whole image was broken.

3. The stone was cut out without human hands. This means that no man had cut it out: it must have been God.

We will now think of what these things mean. If you understand Frames 109 and 114, go to Frame 112.

115   No, the coming King has been chosen by God and the Lord Jesus Christ will rule over the whole world forever. Look again at Frame 117 and you will find the right answer.

116   Yes, Nebuchadnezzar, king of Babylon, was the most glorious, but he was the first of the four, not the last. Read verse 39 carefully and study Frame 112, then pick out the right answer.

117   What was the stone? Read verses 44 and 45. We have seen
that the four different metals speak of four kingdoms which
men set up at different times. In the end God will set up His own
kingdom which will destroy all others and this kingdom will last
forever. The stone is a picture of this. Men did not make this
stone, it was cut out without hands.

Many verses in the Old Testament tell about the great coming
King called the Messiah or the Christ. We will read more about
Christ and His kingdom in Lesson 8. Here we see that He was not
an ordinary man, men did not make Him; He is God, the Son of
God. His kingdom will be greater than any kingdom of men and
He will rule forever.

Which is true?

1.   God has chosen Christ to be the King of the world and
      His kingdom will last forever.   FRAME 111

2.   Men of the world will pick out a great King who will
      rule over the whole world forever.   FRAME 115

3.   If all men were united together, no king could stand up
      against them.   FRAME 120

118   No, God is interested in what is happening and will certainly give glory to His Son when He makes all men bow
before Him. Consider carefully paragraph 2 of Frame 119, then
ask yourself which is the correct answer.

119   God showed Nebuchadnezzar in a dream that there would
be four great kingdoms, then Messiah, God's King, would
come. The first of these kingdoms was Babylon, vs.37,38. There
would be three more before Christ came. We will learn the names
of two of these three kingdoms in Daniel 8 in Lesson 4. We can
learn two very important things about God here in chapter 2.

1. God *knows all things.* He knew what Nebuchadnezzar
dreamed and He could tell Daniel about it. He knew what was
going to happen next and what will happen later on. God knows
the future better than we know the past.

2. God is supreme and *controls all things.* He made Nebuchadnezzar a great king, 2.37, and raised up other great kings after

him, 2.39. In the end He will set up His own Son, the Lord Jesus Christ, to rule forever, v.44.

Now choose the true statement:

1.   God started things when He created the world long ago, but He does not interfere now with what men do.

FRAME 118

2.   God knows the past, but men may choose what they want to do, so God cannot know what will happen in the end.   FRAME 124

3.   God knows all things past and future and He controls men and nations.   FRAME 126

120   Perhaps no human king could stand up against all men, but God's King is the Son of God and He will come with great power. The Stone destroyed **all** the kingdoms of men. Read verse 45 and find the right answer to Frame 117.

121   Daniel was one of 16 prophets of God who wrote the last 17 books of the Old Testament. Many of these prophets wrote about the time when Christ would come, for example, Isaiah:

1. Read Isaiah 40.3 and Matthew 3.3. Isaiah told about John the Baptist who came to prepare the way for Christ.
2. Read Isaiah 42.1 and Matthew 12.18-20. God said He had chosen the Lord Jesus to be the Saviour.
3. Read Isaiah 61.1 and Luke 4.17-19. The Lord Jesus Himself showed that Isaiah wrote about Him and that the Holy Spirit had anointed Him to preach the Good News.
4. Read Isaiah 53.7,8 and Acts 8.32,35. Philip said that Isaiah was speaking about the death of the Lord Jesus.

Many other verses tell about the time when the Lord Jesus came to earth. Everything happened just as God said it would. But some things in the books of the prophets have not yet taken place. We can be sure they will happen when the Lord comes back. The prophets spoke the truth about the first coming of Christ. This helps us to believe and be sure that they spoke the truth about His second coming.

Which of these is true?

1. The prophets said many things, some were true, but others have never taken place, so it is hard to know what to believe.   FRAME 123

2. God's prophets told the truth about Christ's first coming and so we can be sure they told the truth about His return.   FRAME 125

3. Everything the prophets said has already taken place, so we know they told the truth.   FRAME 122

122   No, many things are still future. Read the last part of Frame 121 and find the correct answer, 1 or 2.

123   No, this is not fair; many things took place when Christ came and the rest will surely take place in the future. Read **carefully** the verses in Isaiah and in the New Testament given in Frame 121, and you will see that many details were fulfilled. Look again for the right answer.

124   God has given men the right to choose and does not force anyone to do what is good. However He has kept the power to control the history of all nations. God knows what He is going to do next and certainly has the power to do it. Read Frame 119 again and find the right answer.

125   You are right; go to Frame 127.

126   Yes, this is what the Bible teaches and it is true. Go to Frame 121.

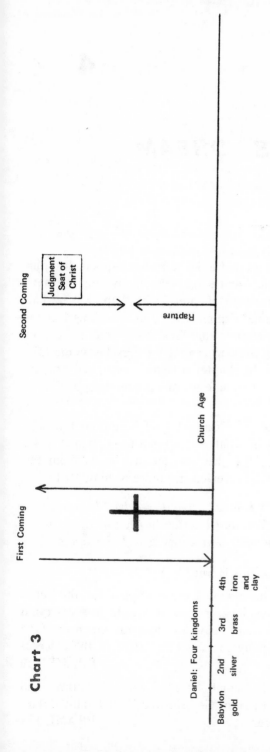

Chart 3

Daniel: Four kingdoms			
Babylon gold	2nd silver	3rd brass	4th iron and clay

First Coming

Second Coming

Church Age

Rapture

Judgment Seat of Christ

127 Now look at Chart 3. Daniel and Nebuchadnezzar lived about 500 years before Christ was born. The kingdom of Babylon was followed by three more kingdoms. God said the fourth kingdom would last until Christ came to destroy it and set up His own kingdom. We know that Christ came, but He has not yet set up His kingdom. When He comes again he will come to rule over all the kingdoms of men. Where is the fourth kingdom today? Let us go on to Lesson 4 and learn more about God's plans for the future. But remember what you need if you want to understand God's ways: you must be separate from the world like Daniel; you must pray for wisdom, and God will give it; you must give glory to God and not become proud. Let us follow Daniel's example. Now turn to Frame 128.

4

DANIEL'S DREAM

128   The first six chapters of Daniel tell what happened to him and his three friends and King Nebuchadnezzar. We have read about the king's dream in chapter 2; in chapter 4 he had another dream, which Daniel explained to him. The king lost his mind for a while until he learned that God is supreme. In chapter 5 Daniel bravely told King Belshazzar that the Persians would take the city and the kingdom. In chapter 6 Daniel continued praying to God and the Lord kept him safe when his enemies put him in with the lions.

Daniel remained true to God and God honoured him and showed him many details of what will happen next. Daniel had a *dream,* 7.1, and a *vision,* 8.1. He also learned more from the Scriptures, 9.2, and then God revealed still more to him, 10.1.

Even Daniel, God's beloved servant, received help when he read the Scripture. You and I certainly need to study the Bible every day to learn what God wants us to know and do.

Which of these statements is true?

1.   Daniel should have shown more respect for the kings. He told Nebuchadnezzar that he would lose his mind and Belshazzar that he would lose his kingdom. God punished Daniel by making him suffer in the place of the lions.   FRAME 129

2.   God honoured Daniel because he was brave and remained true to Him. God showed Daniel many details about the future.   FRAME 131

3.   Daniel did not need to read the Scriptures, because God told him in visions what He wanted him to know.

FRAME 134

129   Wrong. Daniel acted very bravely when he told the kings what God wanted them to know. God did not punish him; He saved him when he was in the place of the lions. Read all of Frame 128 again and find the right answer.

130   Yes, correct, go to Frame 139.

131   Very good. We should always be true to God and obey His commands. Men may not honour us now in this world, but God will be pleased and will honour us when Christ comes. Go to Frame 132.

132   First we will think about Daniel's dream. Read Daniel 7.1-14. Daniel saw four wild animals: a lion, verse 4; a bear, verse 5; a leopard, verse 6; and another animal with ten horns, verse 7. As Daniel watched, another little horn appeared and took the place of three of the ten horns. This wild animal was destroyed, v.11, and the first three animals lost their power, v.12. A Man, the Son of Man, came to rule over all men and nations, vs.13,14.

Answer **all** these four questions:

1.   Who was the king of Babylon when Daniel had his first dream? _____

2.   Which of the four animals had four heads?

_____

Which of the four animals had ten horns?

_____

3.   Which of the four animals got a man's heart or mind?

_____

Which of the four animals had a horn with a man's eyes? _____

4.   How did the Son of Man come? _____

Write in your answers, then check them by turning to Frame 140.

133   Daniel saw this animal in his dream, but the question is, What is it a picture of? We want to know the **meaning** of the dream. Read the last part of Frame 135, then try again.

134   God gave Daniel visions and dreams, but Daniel learned a lot from the book of Jeremiah. Read Daniel 9.2 and the last part of Frame 128, then find the right answer.

135   Let us look at these animals. Read Daniel 7.2-4 again. The *sea* is a picture of the men and nations of this world, always restless, Isaiah 57.20. In the old Hebrew Bible the word *wind* also means spirit and so the wind here speaks of the power of spirits stirring up trouble among men. Four animals came up out of the sea, one at a time.

The first was like a lion. The lion is a strong and brave animal (1 Samuel 1.23), sometimes called the king of animals. The lion in the dream could move very quickly like an eagle, but its wings were pulled off. Then it was given a new heart like a man's heart.

This animal makes us think of King Nebuchadnezzar. He was a king of kings, 2.37, but he became very proud and his heart was changed, 4.16. He lost his mind and lived like an animal for a long time. His hair and fingernails grew very long, like a bird's claws, 4.33. In the end he prayed to God, and got his senses back again, 4.36. This is like the lion in 7.4 who was given a man's heart.

What is the first animal a picture of? Think of these three statements and decide which one is true.

1.   The lion was like King Nebuchadnezzar who set up the first of the great kingdoms which we read about in chapter 2.   FRAME 130

2.   The first animal was like a lion and a bird and a man.
                                                                    FRAME 133

3.   The lion is a strong animal and it could destroy the bear and the leopard.   FRAME 136

136   Your answer is true, but what does the lion stand for? In his dream Daniel did not see the lion destroying other animals. Read Frame 135 and try again.

137   Daniel was wise, but he needed God to help him understand what would happen in the future. Read 7.16 and the second part of Frame 139 again, then choose the right answer.

138   No, not correct. Read verse 25 and paragraph 4 again and find the right answer.

139   The second animal was like a wild bear, which ate a great deal of meat, v.5. The third animal was like a leopard with four wings and four heads. It was given authority to rule, v.6.

Daniel did not understand at first what his dream meant, so he asked someone to explain it, v.16. He learned that these wild animals are pictures of great kings, v.17. We know from chapter 2 that there would be four great kingdoms and Babylon was the first of these. Read Frame 112 again. Belshazzar was the king of the Babylonians or Chaldeans after his grandfather Nebuchadnezzar died. Belshazzar was killed by Darius, king of Media, 5.30,31, so the kingdom of Babylon was followed by the kingdom of Media.

We will learn more about the second and third animals a little later, but first ask yourself if you understand this Frame. Read these three statements and pick out the one which is true:

1.   Daniel was a very wise man and he understood at once that the four animals were pictures of four kingdoms.

FRAME 137

2.   The angel told Daniel that the four wild animals were pictures of four kingdoms. The first was Babylon and the second Media.   FRAME 144

3.   The leopard was a picture of Darius, king of the Medes.

FRAME 142

140   Here are the answers to the questions in Frame 132: 1) Belshazzar, v.1. 2) The third, a leopard, had four heads, and the fourth had ten horns, vs.6,7. 3) The first got a heart or mind like a man's, v.4. The fourth had a horn with eyes like a man's, v.8. 4) The Son of Man came with clouds and with great glory, vs.13,14.

If your answers were all correct, go to Frame 135. If you made a mistake, look at the verses in Daniel 7 again and try to understand.

141   Not quite. The fourth animal is the same as the legs and feet of iron and clay which Nebuchadnezzar saw in his dream. Here the fourth kingdom had ten horns and another little horn which destroyed three of the ten. In Daniel 7 we have learned more details about the fourth and last kingdom. The little horn is only part of the fourth kingdom. Read Frame 143 again and find a better answer.

142   No, the second wild animal, the bear, was a picture of the kingdom of the Medes. We will learn more about the third animal in chapter 8. Read Frame 139 carefully and find the right answer.

143   What about the fourth animal? Read what Daniel saw in his dream, vs.7,8,11,19,20 and then read carefully what the angel said about the fourth animal, vs.23-27. This animal had ten horns and another little horn which could speak proud words, v.8. These eleven horns represent eleven kings, v.24. The little horn came up last and gained the victory over three other kings. This little horn spoke against God and attacked His people, v.25. He was able to change many customs for a short time, but in the end he was destroyed, vs.11,26. This king, called here the *little horn* is very important in the Bible and we will read more about him later.

It is good to know that God controls all the kingdoms of men. Kings and armies may attack His people, but in the end God's Son will surely get the victory.

What does the little horn stand for?

1.   The little horn is the same as the feet of iron and clay in Nebuchadnezzar's dream.   FRAME 141

2.   The little horn is a king who gained victory over ten kings and over the people of God also.   FRAME 149

3.   The little horn is a picture of a great king in the last days who will speak against God and attack His people.

FRAME 150

144   This is correct. Go to Frame 143 and think about the fourth wild animal.

145   Correct. Go to Frame 153.

146   This is true; go on to Frame 157.

147   We saw that the fourth kingdom of Daniel 2 continues until the Lord comes. The stone fell on the feet of the image and destroyed the whole thing, 2.34,35. In Daniel 7 also the fourth kingdom and the little horn continue until Christ comes, vs.21,22. What can we learn about the Lord Jesus Christ in this chapter? Read verses 13 and 14. Daniel saw a Person like the *Son of Man*. The Lord Jesus used this name for Himself many times when He was here on earth. The Son of Man came with the clouds of heaven, and the eternal God, called Ancient of Days, gave Him great authority. The Lord Jesus already has this authority and He said that He will come with clouds, Matthew 24.30; 26.64; 28.18. The Son of Man will rule over the whole world and will share His kingdom with the people of God, vs.14,18,27. We can read these promises again in Revelation 11.15; 20.6; 22.5.

Answer all five questions by writing down the book and chapter and verse in the Old Testament and in the New Testament which proves each statement.

	Old Testament	New Testament
1. The Messiah is called the Son of Man.		
2. God gives Him great authority.		
3. He will come with clouds.		
4. Christ will rule over the whole earth.		
5. God's people will rule with Him.		

When you have written down ten answers, turn to Frame 151 to see if you have answered correctly.

148   Before we leave chapter 7 there are a few more things we should notice about the fourth animal. In later lessons we will try to understand better what these things mean.

1. The fourth animal was **different** from the others, vs.7,19. The first three looked like wild animals which people know, but Daniel did not say that the fourth looked like any particular animal.

2. The little horn of this animal was very proud and spoke big things, vs.8,20, even against God Himself, v.25.

3. He *spoke* against God and *acted* against His people, vs.21,25.

4. He was able to win the fight against God's people for a little while, "A time, and times and half a time," v.25. How long is a *time*? We will ask this question again in Lesson 10, but notice now that the word *times* means more than one, it must mean at least two *times*. So we see that the little horn gets the victory for at least three and a half *times*.

Pick out the true statement:

1. This chapter teaches that the people of God will suffer for 3 1/2 days before the Lord comes to deliver them.
FRAME 152

2. The little horn will win the battle against God's people for 3 1/2 "times", then the Lord will come.
FRAME 145

3. God will kill the little horn when he attacks His people.
FRAME 138

149   No, this little horn will destroy three of the ten kings. He will attack the people of God and gain victory over them for a while. Read Frame 143 again and learn carefully all that Daniel 7 says about the little horn.

150   This is true. Go to Frame 147.

		Old Testament	New Testament
151	1. The Messiah is called the Son of Man	Dan. 7.13	Matt. 24.30
	2. God gives Him great authority	Dan. 7.14	Matt. 28.18
	3. He will come with clouds	Dan. 7.13	Matt. 26.64
	4. Christ will rule over the whole earth	Dan. 7.14	Rev. 11.15
	5. God's people will rule with Him	Dan. 7.18,27	Rev. 20.6; 22.5

How many did you get right? .... If some of your answers were wrong study Frame 147 again until you understand all the answers. Then go to Frame 148.

152   The words 3 1/2 times may mean days or years, but this chapter does not say so. Read Frame 148, paragraph 4, and find a better answer.

153   Daniel had a vision two years after his dream, chapter 8. In his vision Daniel saw two animals, a male sheep and a male goat. The first animal, the ram, had two horns, one higher than the other, v.3. We saw in chapter 7 that four animals were pictures of four kingdoms and the second animal stands for **Media**, Frame 139. Now we read that the ram with the two horns is a picture of the kings of **Media** and **Persia**, v.20. Is the second animal of Daniel 7 the same as the ram of Daniel 8? We do know that the first kingdom, Babylon, continued until the king of **Persia** began to rule, 2 Chronicles 36.20,23. In Daniel 5.31 we read that the kingdom of Babylon continued until Darius the **Mede** took the city and the nation. In Daniel 8 we see that these two nations, Persia and Media, joined together and became a great kingdom. One horn was higher than the other; this stands for Persia and we read more about Persia than Media in the Bible.

Which is true?

1.   The ram is a picture of the second great kingdom, Media and Persia, which rose to power after Babylon.

FRAME 146

2. In chapter 8 Daniel saw a ram which defeated the four animals he saw in chapter 7.   FRAME 156

3. Daniel saw an animal with two horns: the larger one destroyed the smaller one.   FRAME 160

154   No, the goat is the third kingdom (Greece) and the bear is the second kingdom (Media and Persia). Read Frames 153 and 157 again and note that the two animals of chapter 8 are the same as the second and third animals of chapter 7. Look again for the true statement after Frame 157.

155   No, the little horn was a king of part of Alexander's kingdom; **he** attacked the Jews and defiled the temple. Read Frame 161 again and pick out the right answer.

156   No. The fourth kingdom goes on until Christ returns. In chapter 8 the two animals mean the same as the second and third animals in chapter 7. Read Frame 153 again and pick out the true statement.

157   The second animal in Daniel's vision was a male goat. Read Daniel 8.5-8. It had quite a large horn between its eyes and quickly defeated the ram. The goat then became very great, but its horn was soon broken; in its place four large horns grew up.

This goat is a picture of the king of Greece, v.21. We do not read very much about Greece in the Bible, but there is a great deal about it in other old books. Alexander, a great king of Greece, quickly defeated the Persians, but he was a heavy drinker and died at an early age. His kingdom was divided into four parts and each one had its own king for many years, v.22. Remember that the *leopard* had four heads, 7.6.

Which of these is true?

1. The goat in Daniel's vision means the same as the bear in his dream.   FRAME 154

2. The goat is a picture of the third king, the king of Greece. When he died four men took over his kingdom.
                    FRAME 159

3. The four horns on the goat are the same as the ten horns in Daniel 7.7. FRAME 162

158 True, but the little horn of the third kingdom is also a picture of a great leader of the last times. Read the last part of Frame 164 again and choose a better answer.

159 You are right; go on to Frame 161.

160 No, the two horns are two parts of the second kingdom, but one was greater than the other. Read the last part of Frame 153 again, so you can find the right answer.

161 The goat in Daniel's vision had at first a great horn, a picture of Alexander the Great. This horn was broken and four others came up, pictures of four kings who divided up Alexander's kingdom. Another little horn came out of one of the horns and became very great, vs.9-12. This little horn is a picture of a fierce king who lived after these four kings and who ruled over part of Alexander's kingdom. He attacked the land of Israel, called the *pleasant land,* v.9; Ezekiel 20.6. He even defiled the temple of Jehovah and would not let the Jews offer sacrifices to God. In old books of history we read about a wicked king who did all these things; his name was Antiochus Epiphanes.

Pick out the one true statement.

1. Alexander the Great took over the kingdom of Persia and defiled God's temple at Jerusalem. FRAME 155

2. The great horn of the goat is a picture of Antiochus Epiphanes. FRAME 163

3. The little horn in Daniel 8 was a picture of a fierce king of Greece who attacked Israel and stopped the daily sacrifices. FRAME 166

162 No, the goat is a picture of the third kingdom and the animal with ten horns speaks of the fourth kingdom. Read Frame 157 again and find the right answer.

163   The second animal in Daniel's vision had six horns altogether: the great horn, four other horns, and the little horn. It is this little horn which is a picture of Antiochus Epiphanes. Read Frame 161 again and try to understand these six horns, then look for the right answer.

164   We have read about two little horns: in Daniel 7 the little horn was a king of the fourth kingdom and he will attack the people of God until Christ comes to deliver them. In Daniel 8 the little horn was a king of part of the great kingdom of Greece. He also attacked the people of God and the temple of God. Greece was the third kingdom and was replaced by the fourth kingdom before Christ came. So these two little horns live at different times: one long before Christ came and the other one when the Lord comes again.

Yet the angel told Daniel that his vision would be at the time of the end, 8.17,19. Daniel saw in his vision a little horn, a picture of a fierce king who lived after Daniel but before Christ came. This little horn is also a picture of a fierce king of the end times, when Christ comes back again. In Lesson 9 we will learn about some of the leaders of the future.

What about the little horn of Daniel 8? Which statement is the best?

1.   The little horn of the third kingdom lived long before the little horn of the fourth kingdom.   FRAME 158

2.   The eleventh horn of Daniel 7 is the same as the sixth of Daniel 8.   FRAME 167

3.   The little horn in Daniel 8 is a picture of the king of part of Greece and also a picture of a great leader of the future.   FRAME 170

165   This is correct. You may go to Frame 169.

166   You are right, go to Frame 164.

167   These are both called little horns, but they belong to different kingdoms and live at different times. However the little horn of the goat is a picture of a man who will rise up in the last times. Study Frame 164 again and find the right answer.

168   We have seen that the little horn of Daniel 8.9 was a picture of Antiochus Epiphanes. This wicked man was king of Syria, a part of the kingdom of Greece which is north of Israel. This man fought with Israel and entered the temple of Jehovah. He made the temple unclean when he offered up pigs as sacrifices to his own gods. This terrible sin is called the *desolation* and it lasted for 2,300 days, over six years, v.14. After that time God gave the Jews enough power to get control of the temple and make it clean again. Other verses in Daniel speak of times and weeks and days. We will study these in Lesson 10 and also learn more about the *desolation*.

Which is true?

1.   Antiochus Epiphanes, king of Syria, made God's temple unclean for about 6 1/2 years.   FRAME 165

2.   Daniel had this vision about 553 years before Christ. If every day is equal to a year, 2,300 years after the vision would be the year 1747. Something very important happened then.   FRAME 171

3.   Jehovah is the God of the whole earth and anyone can offer any kind of sacrifice to his own god at the temple of Jehovah.   FRAME 174

169   We know from Daniel the names of the first three kingdoms: Babylon, Media and Persia, and Greece. What about the fourth kingdom? The Old Testament does not tell us the name of the fourth kingdom, but in the New Testament we find that **Rome** ruled over all countries. You can find the names of three great kings of Rome in Luke 2.1; 3.1; Acts 11.28. We also know from other old books that Rome gained the victory over Greece soon after the time of Antiochus Epiphanes and continued to rule the world until long after the days of Peter and Paul and John.

Now you can write in the names of four kingdoms and four kings.

	Daniel 2	Daniel 7	Daniel 8	Name of Kingdom	Name of one king
1.	Gold	Lion			
2.	Silver	Bear	Ram		
3.	Brass	Leopard	Goat		
4.	Iron & clay	Wild animal with 10 horns			

When you have written in eight names, turn to Frame 175 to see if you got the right answers.

170   This is the best answer. Go to Frame 168.

171   Many people think that a day means a year, but the Bible does not say so and anyway, we should not try to set any dates. Read what Frame 168 says and get the right answer.

172   These four kingdoms lasted for many years; these years are called the *times of the Gentiles*. Heathen kings have ruled over the land of Israel ever since the days of Jeremiah and Daniel. Jeremiah said that God would give Babylon the victory over Israel and Nebuchadnezzar, king of Babylon, would destroy Jerusalem, Jeremiah 21.7; 22.26; 32.28; 52.4. Daniel said that three other kingdoms would follow Babylon and the fourth would last until Christ comes. How long will the time of the Gentiles last? The Lord Jesus Himself said that heathen people would control Jerusalem until the time of the Gentiles is up. Then Christ will return with great power and glory, Luke 21.24,27.

We will see that the time of the Gentiles may soon be over. Then the great period of God's grace will come to an end. It is good to know that we are on God's side, but we ought to warn others about what will happen next.

Ask yourself which of these statements is true.
1.   The fourth kingdom, Rome, came to an end long ago, so the time of the Gentiles is over.   FRAME 173
2.   The time of the Gentiles started with Nebuchadnezzar and will last until Christ comes again.   FRAME 177

3.   God loved people of all nations and always will. We cannot say that a particular time belongs to the Jews or to the Gentiles.   FRAME 176

173   The fourth kingdom came to an end, but other Gentile nations continue to rule over Jerusalem. Read again what the Lord said in Luke 21.24-27, also read Frame 172 again, then find the right answer.

174   Jehovah is God of the whole earth, but only those who believed in Him were allowed to go into the temple yard, and they could offer only those sacrifices which were according to the law. Antiochus Epiphanes forced his way into the temple and broke God's law, a terrible sin. Go back to Frame 168 and find the right answer.

175   The four kingdoms are: 1. Babylon; 2. Media and Persia; 3. Greece; 4. Rome.   Here are the names of some of the kings: Babylon: Nebuchadnezzar, Belshazzar, Frame 128; Media and Persia: Darius, Cyrus, Frame 153; Greece: Alexander, Frame 157; Rome: Augustus, Tiberius, Claudius, Frame 171.

You were only asked to give the name of one king for each kingdom, but if your answer was wrong, look at the Frame numbers given and be sure you understand, then go to Frame 172.

176   Yes, God loves all men, but He greatly blessed His people Israel in the past and will do so again in the future. Read Frame 172, this will help you to find the right answer.

177   This is true. Now read Frame 178.

178   Now look at Chart 4. It is like Chart 3, but we can now add a few details. We can see that the time of the Gentiles started with the king of Babylon and goes on until Christ comes again. Media and Persia were important for a while, then Greece. Rome continued until the Lord Jesus came the first time. At the end a great king will rise up and attack God's people, but the Lord will destroy him when He comes.

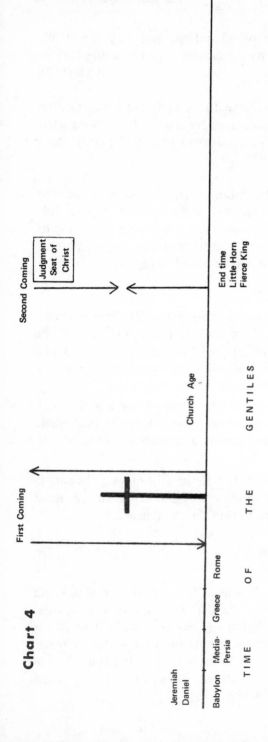

Chart 4

First Coming   **Second Coming**

Jeremiah
Daniel

Babylon   Media-Persia   Greece   Rome

Judgment Seat of Christ

Church Age

End time
Little Horn
Fierce King

TIME   OF   THE   GENTILES

The little horn of the fourth animal is a picture of this great king, Frame 143. The angel told Daniel that a fierce king would rise up in the end time, who would speak against God and attack His people, but he will be destroyed by the Lord, Frame 164.

Study this chart and notice especially what we have added to Chart 3. When you understand the Chart, go on to Lesson 5 and Frame 179.

WHEN WILL

5

THESE THINGS BE ?

179   Of course, we do not know when all these things will take
place and no one should set a date or claim that he knows
what will happen next. The Bible teaches that no man can know
when the Lord will come, and the Father keeps this authority for
Himself, Acts 1.7. However, we can and should and must study
very carefully what the Bible does say about the future.

We have seen that the Lord promised to come back and take
His people to be with Himself. Dead Christians will rise to life and
we will be taken up into the air to meet the Lord in the clouds.
When will this take place? God gave Daniel information about the
time of the Gentiles when four kingdoms would follow one after
another, Babylon, Media and Persia, Greece, and Rome. At the
end of the last kingdom a fierce king will rule and attack God's
people. He will be destroyed when the Lord comes.

The time of the **Gentiles** has already lasted for hundreds of
years, for many centuries. Let us now think about the **Jews** and
what the Lord Jesus taught in Matthew 24 about His coming
again. (There are no questions for this Frame; go on to Frame
180.)

180   Who are the Jews? Long ago God promised Abraham that
his family would become very large and He would greatly
bless his descendants, Genesis 12.2,3. Later He promised David
that his Descendant will rule as King over Israel forever, 2 Samuel
7.11,12,13,16. But the people of Israel forgot God and sinned
against Him. Finally the nation became so wicked that God

punished them very severely. He allowed the first king of Babylon to burn Jerusalem and take away the people as prisoners for seventy years, Jeremiah 25.8-11.

The Jews repented and God commanded the first king of Persia to let them go back again to their land, Ezra 1.1-3. At last the Messiah came, but the Jews refused to accept Him. They killed the Lord Jesus and God again forced them to leave their country.

What about God's promises to Abraham and David? God must punish His people when they sin, but He cannot break His own promises, Hebrews 6.13,14,18. We can be sure that God will yet bless His people Israel. The time of the Gentiles will come to an end, the Lord Jesus will come and rule as King over Israel and the whole world.

Which of these statements is true?

1.   God promised to bless Abraham's descendants and He has never punished the people of Israel for their sins.

FRAME 183

2.   Israel has sinned many times and refused their own Messiah, so God's promises to Israel will be fulfilled when He blesses the Church.   FRAME 185

3.   God has punished Israel for the sins of the nation, but some day He will yet fulfill all His promises to Abraham and David.   FRAME 187

181   No, the Lord taught in Matthew 24 that the Jews will have a time of terrible trouble just before He returns. Read the last part of Frame 182. Then look for the right answer.

182   God called Israel His own people and the Jews are very important in God's plan. The Lord Jesus was born in the nation of Israel, a Descendant of David and Abraham, Matthew 1.1; Romans 9.4,5. In Matthew 24 the Lord was speaking to His disciples, all Jews. Read Matthew 24.1-3. They left the temple and walked from the city of Jerusalem to the Mount of Olives. From there they could see Jerusalem, the holy city of the Jews; they could also see the temple, their place of worship.

The Lord told His disciples that the temple would be totally destroyed, v.2. Then they asked Him two questions:

1. When will these things be? When will the temple be destroyed?

2. What is the sign of your coming at the end of the age?

The Lord answered the first question about the temple, and Luke tells us what He said, Luke 21.20-24. We know from old books of history that the temple was destroyed in the year 70, about 40 years after the Lord said these words. Here in Matthew the Lord told them the signs of His coming at the end of the age. Most of these signs will be terrible trouble for the Jewish people. First there is: the beginning of Pain, Matthew 24.4-8;

then the Great Tribulation, vs.9-22;

then the coming of the Son of Man, vs.23-31.

The disciples were not afraid to ask the Lord to help them to understand. This is our privilege also. God has told us to ask for wisdom, and He has promised to give it to us, James 1.5. As you read this book, ask the Lord to help you understand His Word.

Which of these statements is true?

1. There will be peace in the world and the Jews will be rich and happy when the Lord comes.   FRAME 181

2. After Christ comes there will be a time of terrible trouble in the world.   FRAME 184

3. The disciples were Jews and the Lord told them that the signs of His coming will be terrible trouble for the Jews.   FRAME 188

183   No, God is holy and He **must** punish His people when they sin against Him. Read the last part of Frame 180 again and look for the right answer.

184   This chapter teaches that the Great Tribulation will end when the Lord comes. Read Frame 182 again and try to get the right answer.

185   No, God cannot change His own promises. He will bless the Church and He will bless the Jews too, after He has punished them for breaking His law. Study Frame 180 again and look for the right answer.

186 The Beginning of Pain

Read Matthew 24.4-8. Here we have four signs of the end of the age:

1.   Many men will say "I am Christ", but they will be lying. Still thousands will believe them and follow them, v.5.
2.   There will be many wars before the end of the age, v.6.
3.   Many people will be very hungry, v.7.
4.   The world will shake in different places and make people afraid, v.7.

There have always been wars, famines, and earthquakes, and even in early days there were many false leaders who lied to the people, Matthew 7.15; Acts 5.36,37; 1 John 2.18; 4.1. But these things will get worse, and happen more often, before the Lord comes. Yet these things are only the beginning of Pain.

The Lord spoke about false christs, wars, famines and earthquakes. Will these things be signs that the end of the age is drawing near? Which of these statements is true?

1.   These signs will be seen more often than at present, but worse things will follow.   FRAME 191

2.   When these things happen, men will know that the age is over.   FRAME 193

3.   These things have always been common and the world still goes on, so they will not prove that the end is near.   FRAME 195

187   This is true. Go to Frame 182.

188   You are right, go to Frame 186.

189   This is true, vs.14,17, but go to Frame 192 again and consider statements 2 and 3.

190   No, God will save many Jews who believe in Christ and they will be alive when He comes. Read verse 13 and Frame 204 again, then look for the right answer.

191   This is correct. Now you may go on to Frame 192.

192   The Great Tribulation
1. Next we read about the Great Tribulation, Matthew 24.9-22. This will be a time of terrible trouble for all men, especially for the Jews. Notice:

1) All men will hate those who believe in Christ, vs.9,10.

2) False prophets will teach what is not true, v.11.

3) Some believers will lose their love for the Lord because there will be so much evil in the world, v.12. Others will continue to serve the Lord to the end of that time of trouble. They will still be alive when the Lord comes, v.13.

4) Many will love the Lord and will preach the Good News in the whole world, v.14.

5) The Jews in the land of Israel will have to run away, vs.15-20. The Lord advised them to go out as quickly as they could. They should not even wait long enough to get extra clothes. Pregnant women will have special difficulty and it will be worse still if they have to run away in the winter time or on a sabbath day.

What will it be like in the days of the Great Tribulation? Think of these three statements and decide which is or are true (more than one statement may be true).

1.   Some Jews will go and preach the Good News in all the world, and others will stay in Judea until they have to run away very quickly.   FRAME 189

2.   Some will be killed, but others will believe the false prophets.   FRAME 194

3.   People of all nations will have a chance to hear about the Kingdom, but most of them will hate those who believe.   FRAME 198

193   Men have always suffered from these things, but when
these signs become worse, and happen more often, men
can know that they are getting near the end of the age, but not the
very end. Read verse 8 and Frame 186 again, then look for the
right statement.

194   This is true, vs.9,11, but go back to Frame 192 and think
about statements 1 and 3.

195   These things have always been common, but the Lord said
they were signs of the end. They will become much more
common near the end, but still worse things must come. Read
Frame 186 and try again to choose the right answer.

196   The Lord Jesus gave His followers an important sign and
told them to run away as soon as possible when they see
this sign. This is called the Abomination of Desolation or the
Awful Horror, and it will stand in the holy place, Matthew 24.15.
What does it mean? Daniel spoke about this and we are told to
understand these words.

The holy place means God's holy temple. Daniel spoke about
the Abomination of Desolation in Daniel 9.27; 11.31; 12.11.
Daniel said the *little horn* would stop the Jews from offering
sacrifices to God, Daniel 8.11. If you do not remember, read
Frame 161 and 168 again. A Greek king called Antiochus
Epiphanes did this and he is a picture of a great leader of the
future who will do the same. This person will make God's holy
altar unclean and prevent the Jews from offering their sacrifices to
Jehovah. After that this leader will start to attack God's people
and so the Lord Jesus told them to get away as soon as possible
because the Great Tribulation was very near.

What is the Abomination of Desolation the sign of?

1.   A king will make God's temple unclean and prevent the
Jews from offering sacrifices to Jehovah.   FRAME 199

2.   The Abomination of Desolation is a sign that the Great
Tribulation will start at once.   FRAME 201

3.   This is the Awful Horror, a sign that the Rapture is near.
FRAME 202

197   This is true. Go on to Frame 208.

198   This is true, vs.9,14, but you should see that all **three** statements are true. If you thought some were wrong go to Frame numbers given and read verses 9, 11, 14 and 17 again. Then go to Frame 196.

199   Yes, this is the Abomination of Desolation, but what is it a **sign** of? Read Frame 196 again and ask yourself what is the Abomination of Desolation a sign of.

200   The first time the Lord came, He sent His disciples to preach the Good News, but the second time He will come with great power and glory. You should read Frame 208 once more and find the right answer.

201   True, the Lord told His followers to run away at once when they see the Abomination of Desolation in the holy place at Jerusalem. Go on to Frame 204.

202   No, the Lord Jesus did not teach anything about the Rapture in this chapter. Later the Holy Spirit told Paul about the Rapture. You should read Frame 196 again and look more carefully for the right answer.

203   No, all men will be affected and if God did not shorten this time, all would be killed. Read verse 22 and try again.

204   So the Great Tribulation will start with the Abomination of Desolation. This will be the worst time of trouble which men have ever had and millions of people will be killed, Matthew 24.21. How long will it last?

     God will in mercy reduce the time; if He didn't, all men would die. But God has chosen that many people will be saved and it is not His will that all men should die in the Great Tribulation, v.22. We will learn more about the Great Tribulation in Lesson 10 and we will find out how long it will last. In Matthew 24 we see that the Great Tribulation will last until Christ comes.

Which of these four statements is true?

1.   The Great Tribulation will start with the Abomination of Desolation and end after a short time when the Lord comes.   FRAME 197

2.   The Great Tribulation will be a time of terrible trouble for all Jews, but it will not affect the Gentiles.

FRAME 203

3.   The Great Tribulation will be the worst time of trouble up to then, but there will be worse things still after that in the future.   FRAME 207

4.   In the Great Tribulation all Jews who believe in Christ will be killed.   FRAME 190

205   You are right, go on to Frame 211.

206   No, most men will weep when they see Christ because they will not accept Him as their Saviour. Read Matthew 24.30 and Revelation 1.7 again. Then find the right answer.

207   The Great Tribulation will be the worst time of trouble in the history of mankind; there will never be anything so bad on earth after that. Read verse 21 again and Frame 204, then look for the right answer.

208   **The Coming of the Son of Man**
         Then the Lord Jesus told about His return to earth. Everyone will know when Christ comes. Read Matthew 24.23-31. Before He comes many will stand up and say "I am the Messiah" and some of them will perform great signs and miracles. These false prophets will be able to persuade millions of people to follow them and they would like to make God's people believe in them too. So the Lord warned His disciples not to follow anyone; when the Lord Jesus comes, everyone will know at once that He is here.
         The sun and moon and stars will grow dark and the Lord will come like a great flash of lightning filling the whole sky. He will come on the clouds, with power and glory. The angels will gather His people who have been scattered all over the earth.

Which of these statements is true?

1.   When the Lord comes back He will soon get a few disciples who will go out and preach the Good News to all people.   FRAME 200

2.   False christs will perform many miracles, but when the true Christ comes in glory, everyone will know who He is.   FRAME 205

3.   The Lord told His disciples to consider the claims of all who say they are Christ, and decide which one is true.
                                                    FRAME 210

209   You are right. Go on to Frame 216.

210   No, He told His disciples not to follow them nor to believe in them. Read verses 23 and 26 again. Then look for the right answer after Frame 208.

211   We see that the Lord will come very suddenly. Most people of the world will weep when Christ comes, v.30, Revelation 1.7, but those who believe will be very happy when they see the Lord. The Bible tells us some of the things which will happen before Christ comes. Still many people will not believe or get ready even when they see these signs.

So the Lord gave another lesson, vs.32,33. In the land of Israel you can tell when summer is near because the trees start to put out their leaves, especially the fig tree. We should also understand today that the time is near for Christ to return. The Lord has told us, His followers, that He will come back, Frame 5.

We do not see the signs promised by the Lord in Matthew 24 but we can see what is happening in the world today. Everything is getting ready for the events which will take place just as the Lord said they would. So we can know that the time is near.

Which of these is true?

1.   All men will be very happy when they see the Lord.
                                                    FRAME 206

2.   God has given many signs to warn people but still millions will weep when they see the Lord come suddenly to this world.   FRAME 209

3.   Christ will come like lightning and both Jews and Gentiles, believers and unbelievers, will be completely surprised.   FRAME 214

212   This is correct. Go to Frame 220.

213   The Lord has told us many things and when these happen we can be sure His coming is getting nearer. Read Frame 220 and pick out the right answer.

214   Both Jews and Gentiles who believe God's Word will know that Christ's coming is very near, so they will not be completely surprised. Read Frame 211 and try again for the right answer.

215   True, go right on to Frame 224.

216   The Lord Jesus told a story about a fig tree in Luke 13.6-9. It did not produce any figs, so the owner said to cut it down. But the gardener asked him to leave it for one more year and he agreed to this.

This is a picture of Israel. God was going to judge this nation if the people did not turn from their sins. He did judge Israel in the year 70; see Frame 182. The Lord taught this lesson the second time in Matthew 21.19.

Which of these statements is true?

1.   In the New Testament the fig tree is a picture of Israel.
                    FRAME 212

2.   Israel turned from their sin and God forgave them.
                    FRAME 218

3.   The Lord taught that Israel would never be blessed again.   FRAME 222

217   No, the sun, moon and stars become dark before Christ comes in power and glory and this takes place after the Rapture. Read again Frame 224 and look for the right statement.

218   The nation of Israel has never repented of their sin of rejecting Christ, but later on they will do so. Try again for the right answer.

219   You can be ready to meet the Lord if you have received Him as your Saviour. If you are not sure, just remember that God loves you and Christ died for you. Believe this message from the Bible and accept the Lord Jesus in your heart. He will be glad to accept you and take you to heaven when He comes. If this Frame makes you happy, go on to Frame 230.

220   In Matthew 24.32 we see that the fig tree will put out green leaves just before the summer comes. Is there anything to show us that the Lord will soon come again? This chapter teaches us that Jews will be living in Jerusalem just before the Lord comes. They will be offering sacrifices to Jehovah in their temple. The Lord Jesus taught that a wicked man will stop them from offering sacrifices, and then they should run away from Jerusalem as quickly as possible, 24.15,16. The Jews were driven from their land in the year 70 and did not get control of it again until 1948. Later still in 1967 they got control of Jerusalem but could not build their own temple again. However, we see these changes in Israel and they show us that God is preparing the world for the return of His Son.

Read the following statements carefully and decide which one is true.

1.   The Lord said He would come suddenly and so we should not look for signs.   FRAME 213

2.   The Lord said that Israel would be in their land before He returns and we can see that this is true today.
        FRAME 215

3.   For 1,878 years Israel did not control their land, but now everything prophesied in Matthew 24 has been fulfilled.   FRAME 225

221   The Scripture teaches that certain things will happen at the Rapture and different things when Christ comes in power and glory. Read Frame 224 again and you will find the right answer.

222   The Lord did say that no fruit would grow on the fig tree and most of the people of Israel at that time died without repenting, Frame 180. However, the Bible teaches that Israel will repent in the future. Read Frame 216 again and look for the right answer.

223   1. The beginning of Pain. 2. The Abomination of Desolation. 3. The Great Tribulation. 4. Christ comes. 5. The judgment of all living men. If you did not get all these answers correctly, look up the verses in Matthew 24 and 25 again. When you understand them clearly, go on to Lesson 6, Frame 238.

224   In Matthew 24 the Lord Jesus taught us many things about the Jews and the Gentiles, but what about the Church, the believers who are alive today? We have seen that the Lord will come with a shout and dead Christians will rise first. The Lord will take us up into the clouds where we will meet Him. From then on we will be forever with the Lord, 1 Thessalonians 4.17; Frame 63.

In Matthew 24 it is quite different. The sun, moon and stars will become dark and the Lord will come with power and glory like a flash of lightning. Matthew 24 and 1 Thessalonians 4 both teach about the time when the Lord will come, but these chapters must speak about different times. We will see that the Rapture of the Church will take place **before** Christ comes in power and glory.

Consider these three statements and decide which one is right.

1.   Before the Rapture, the sun, moon and stars will become dark.   FRAME 217

2.   The Rapture will take place at the same time as Christ's coming in glory.   FRAME 221

3.   Matthew 24 and 1 Thessalonians 4 both teach about the coming of Christ, but they are different; one tells about the Rapture of the Church and the other about Christ coming in power and glory.   FRAME 229

225   Not everything. For example, the Abomination of
Desolation has not happened yet, but the Jews are back in
control of Jerusalem and the land of Israel. Read Frame 220
carefully and find the right answer.

226   No, read verse 28 again and look for a better answer.

227   No, dead believers will rise at the Rapture, Frame 42. Only
living people will be judged when Christ comes and the
Lord did not speak in this chapter about anyone rising from death.
We will see later that wicked men will rise from death a thousand
years after this. Read Frame 233 again and pick out the correct
answer.

228   The Ten Young Women
    In the next chapter the Lord told a story about ten
young women. Read Matthew 25.1-11. These young women fell
asleep while waiting for the bridegroom to come for the wedding.
When he came he found only five of them were really ready to
meet him.

    The Lord Jesus told this story to teach us that we should be
ready for Him, because we do not know the exact time when He
will come. Many people do not even know that the Lord will
return, others do not understand that He is coming soon. We know
that He is coming back but we do not know the exact time. We
can see many things happening in the world today and we should
be ready to meet Him when He comes. Read also Matthew
24.36-51.

    There is only one question for this Frame: *Are you ready if
the Lord should come today? Think about this, then go to
Frame 219.*

229   True, you may go to Frame 228.

230   Then the Lord told another story, about three servants.
Their master gave each of them some money and then
went away for a long time. When he came back he was happy to
find that two of them had served him well while he was away.

When He returns the Lord Jesus will call us each one to see what we have done while He was away. Some have served Him well and He will tell everyone in heaven about this. We have seen in Frame 84 that all believers will stand before the Judgment Seat of Christ. Some believers will receive crowns or rewards. The Lord will praise some believers because they have done well. This will make them very happy in heaven.

Pick out the one statement which is true.

1.   The man told his three servants to keep the money he had given them.   FRAME 226

2.   In heaven the Lord will tell all who are there that they have done well in this world.   FRAME 231

3.   The Lord will give honour to His people who have served Him well while He was away.   FRAME 235

231   The Lord always told the truth and of course in heaven no one can say what is not true. The Lord Jesus will say these words only about those who have served Him well while He was away. Go back to Frame 230 and try again.

232   No, believers will go to heaven at the Rapture. Read Frame 61. In Matthew 25 believers enter the Kingdom and stay here on earth. Read verse 34 and the second paragraph of Frame 233. Then look again for the right answer.

233   The Judgment Seat of Christ will take place soon after the Rapture and only believers will be there. But after the Lord comes in power and glory He will gather all the people who are still alive in the world and they will be judged. Read Matthew 25.31-46. We see that the Lord will divide all men into two groups like a shepherd who separates the sheep from the goats.

The believers are like the sheep; they will stand on the right side of the Lord, and the others on the left. Those on the right have shown that they believed in Christ by being kind to His people. During the Great Tribulation, the Jews will have to run away when their enemies try to kill them. The sheep are believers who will enter the kingdom of Christ and live here in this world.

The unbelievers are like the goats; they stand on the left side of the Lord. They showed that they did not believe in Christ because they would not help His people, the Jews. These unbelievers must go to the place which is prepared for Satan.

Now consider these three statements and choose the one which is right.

1. All dead men will rise and stand before Christ and He will decide whether they are like sheep or goats.
    FRAME 227

2. When Christ comes in power and glory, all believers on earth will go to heaven.   FRAME 232

3. The Lord will gather all people who are still alive on earth and will divide true believers from unbelievers.
    FRAME 234

234   True, go to Frame 237.

235   This is correct, go to Frame 233.

236   Which of these five things comes first? Write it down at the right after number 1. Then write down all the others in the proper order. If you are not sure, look at Chart 5.

The Abomination of Desolation. 1. _____

The beginning of Pain.   2. _____

Christ comes in power and glory. 3. _____

The Great Tribulation.   4. _____

The Judgment of living men.   5. _____

When you have written in your answers turn to Frame 223 to see if you got them all right.

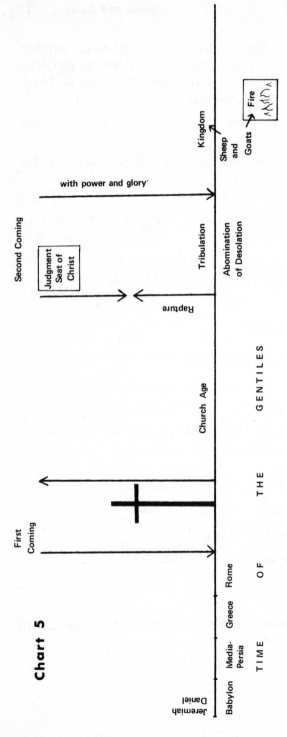

Chart 5

First Coming

Second Coming

with power and glory

Judgment Seat of Christ

Rapture

Church Age

Tribulation

Abomination of Desolation

Kingdom

Sheep and Goats → Fire

Babylon   Media-Persia   Greece   Rome

TIME   OF   THE   GENTILES

Jeremiah Daniel

237 Now look at Chart 5. The Rapture is quite different from Christ's coming in power and glory. Before the Lord comes there will be Great Tribulation, especially after the Abomination of Desolation occurs. The Great Tribulation will end when the Lord comes to the world with power and glory. Then He will judge all living people. Those who believed in Him will enter the Kingdom. All others must go to the fire which God prepared for the devil.

Look up all these things on Chart 5. When you understand them go to Frame 236.

6

THE CHURCH AGE

238   We have seen that the Lord Jesus will come back and take His Church out of this world and we will go home to heaven. We have looked at some of the great Bible chapters on Prophecy, John 14, 1 Thessalonians 4, Daniel 2, 7 and 8, Matthew 24, 25. Let us now look at Revelation 1-3 and ask what we can learn about the Church. But we may first ask what is the Church?

In Ephesians we read that the Church is like a body: Christ is the Head and we are members, Ephesians 4.15; 5.30. The Church is also like a man's bride or wife: Christ loves the Church and takes care of it, Ephesians 5.25-27.

The Church is different from Israel, 1 Corinthians 10.32, although Jews who believe become members of the true Church, the Body of Christ. The Church is made up of all who trust Christ *at this time*. It is clear that the Church has a special place in God's plans.

Which of these three statements is true?

1.   The Church today is no different from all believers of any other age.   FRAME 242

2.   The Church is like the Body or Bride of Christ and it has a special place in God's plan.   FRAME 244

3.   Many Jews are saved today and they will go to heaven, but they are not members of the Body of Christ.
                              FRAME 247

239   You are wrong on both points. It is true that John the Baptist taught people to repent and to be baptized. Some of them followed the Lord Jesus and became members of the Church when the Holy Spirit came down. These men were believers, but they did not become one Body until the Holy Spirit came to live in them, on the day of Pentecost.

It is also wrong to say that only baptized people belong to the true Church. The Holy Spirit puts all believers into the Church when they are born again. Read Frame 241 more carefully and study all the verses mentioned in it. Then look for the right answer.

240   The Church has made many mistakes in its history and we cannot safely find answers to our problems except in the New Testament. Look for a true statement.

241   When did the Church start? We have seen that the Church is the Body of Christ and all true believers are members. Before the Lord Jesus went back to heaven, He promised His followers that they would be baptized with the Holy Spirit in a few days, and so they were, on the day of Pentecost, Acts 1.5; 2.4. The Holy Spirit came on many believers and He made these people into one body, the Church. The Church was first formed on the day of Pentecost and all who believe today are added to the same Body, 1 Corinthians 12.13.

Many believers have died and others have been killed, but the Church is still alive and active. It will be here until the Rapture when Christ comes to take every believer to heaven. The time from the day of Pentecost to the Rapture is called the Church Age.

Think about these things and then choose the right answer.

1.   The Church was started by John the Baptist and everyone must be baptized to enter the Church.
FRAME 239

2.   The Church began on the day of Pentecost and will remain on earth until the Rapture.   FRAME 248

3.   After the Rapture the Church will no longer exist.
FRAME 250

242 Wrong. The Church has a special place in God's plan and the Bible says the Church is the Body of Christ. Read the second part of Frame 238 again and find the right answer.

243 Christ is in heaven but He is the Son of God and has promised to be with us always, Matthew 18.20; 28.20. Read Frame 252 again, also Revelation 1.10-20; then look for the right answer.

244 This is right; go next to Frame 241.

245 The book of Acts tells how the Church began and spread, and the book of Revelation tells us about the Lord's coming. Between Acts and Revelation there are 21 letters written by Paul, Peter, James, John and Jude. The Holy Spirit led God's servants to write these 21 letters to churches and individuals, and God has shown us in these letters what the churches should do. The New Testament is the only book we have to show us what God wants us to do in the Church Age.

The early churches in Galatia, Corinth, Philippi and Colossae had great problems and Paul through the Holy Spirit told them what to do. All churches since then have had many problems and we still have many today. We can turn to the New Testament and ask God to show us what to do.

Christ is still the Head of the Church which is His Body. He is also the Head of every church, large or small, if the people love Him. Every church ought to obey His Word and follow the New Testament.

Which of these four statements is true?

1. The Church is more than 1,900 years old, so we can find the answer to our problems in old books of Church history.   FRAME 240

2. In the New Testament God has given us enough information to guide us in all church problems today.
                                                          FRAME 246

3. In time of difficulty, all we need is to pray.
                                                          FRAME 251

4.   Paul taught the early churches what to do, but this is no help to us in the great problems we have to face in the modern church today.   FRAME 253

246   True. The New Testament gives us the general principle or law and the Holy Spirit will show us just what to do to please the Lord. Now go to Frame 252.

247   This is wrong; all people saved at this time are members of the Church which is Christ's Body. Read Ephesians 2.14 and the second part of Frame 238. Then look for the right answer.

248   This is true; go to Frame 245.

249   This is true and very important. Go to Frame 257.

250   After the Rapture the Church will no longer be on earth but it will exist in heaven. God will get glory through the Church through eternity forever, Ephesians 3.21. Go back to Frame 241 and find the right answer.

251   Indeed we must pray, but we must also learn from the New Testament what God says. Read Frame 245 and try again.

252   Everyone's body has a head which guides and controls the body. Christ is the Head of the Body which is His Church, Ephesians 1.22,23; 4.15. In Revelation 1 we see Christ standing as the Leader among the seven churches. Read Revelation 1.10-20.

The apostle John saw someone who looked like a man, v.13, but who really was God, the First and Last, v.17; Isaiah 44.6. He had been dead but had risen from death, v.18. This person was the Lord Jesus, both Son of God and Son of Man, who died and rose again. John saw Him standing among the seven lamp-stands which were pictures of the seven churches, v.20. The Lord held seven stars in His right hand; these stand for the angels or messengers of the seven churches. These verses teach us that Christ should be in control of all His churches.

Consider these three statements:

1. Christ is the Head of the Church, but He is in heaven and wants each church to guide its own affairs.

   FRAME 243

2. Christ is standing among the churches and watches what we do and wants to keep control of all things.

   FRAME 249

3. John saw a great man whom Christ put in control over His churches.   FRAME 258

253   Problems today are about the same as those which the Church had in New Testament times. Some men today think they are so wise they do not need the New Testament but they will surely make mistakes. The only way we can please God is to follow His Word, the Bible. Read Frame 245 and look for the right answer.

254   The Lord told John to write to the leader because many of the believers could not read. However, the Lord's message was for all believers. For example, He promised to give a great reward to anyone who wins the victory, 2.7. Read the first part of Frame 257. Then look again for the right answer.

255   No, they soon lost their first love for Christ, as the church of Ephesus did. Read paragraph 1 of Frame 260 and look up the verses given there; then try again for the right answer.

256   This is correct, but you should read the other statements after Frame 263 to see if any others are true.

257   Where were these seven churches, 1.4,11? The province of Asia was part of the Roman Empire; today it is called Turkey. Each of these seven churches had different problems and the Lord sent a little message to each one. The letter was sent to a leader in each church, but the message was for all the people.

   These messages are for us today also. There are churches today with the same conditions as those which the Lord saw in Ephesus. He gives them the same message. Other churches are like Smyrna or Philadelphia or Laodicea. These churches should listen to what the Holy Spirit says.

Pick out the right statement.

1.   John wrote seven letters to the leaders of seven churches and told them what to do for the people.

FRAME 254

2.   These messsages for seven churches long ago have no value for our churches today.   FRAME 259

3.   There are some churches today like each of the seven churches of Asia and the Lord's message is just as important as when John first wrote this book.

FRAME 261

258   No, Christ wants to keep control of the churches for Himself. John saw a man who is also the Son of God, the Man Christ Jesus. Read verses 17 and 18 and Frame 252, then find the right answer.

259   The Bible is the Word of God and God's truth is for all people at all times. The Lord speaks through His Word and we can certainly learn what He wants us to do. Read the second paragraph of Frame 257 and try again.

260   These messages in Revelation 2 and 3 are for us today. Even in John's time there were many churches like the church of Ephesus. The believers had lost their first love for Christ. In the beginning the church was very busy praising the Lord and telling people about Christ, Acts 2.46,47; 8.4. But later the believers were fighting and quarreling among themselves, 1 Corinthians 1.11; Philippians 4,2,3. They did not love the Lord as they did at first.

Later the churches went through a time of terrible trouble. Old books of history show us that many Christians were thrown into prison, but most of them were faithful to the Lord, even though their enemies killed some of them. These churches were like the church of Smyrna, 2.8-11.

We can read about the history of the churches through the

Church Age from the day of Pentecost to the present time. There are seven periods in the Church Age and the Church in each period was like one of the seven churches of Revelation 2 and 3. We will study the Lord's messages to these churches and we will see that they are like the different periods in the Church Age.

Which of these statements is true?

1. As long as the apostles lived, the early Christians continued to love and serve the Lord just as they did at the beginning. FRAME 255

2. The seven churches in Asia were like the whole Church at different times through the Church Age. FRAME 262

3. The churches in the New Testament went through a great deal of trouble, just as the church of Smyrna did. FRAME 266

261 This is correct; go to Frame 260.

262 This is true. Go to Frame 263.

263 The first letter was sent to the church of Ephesus. Read Revelation 2.1-7. The Lord Jesus saw many good things in this church, vs.2,3. The believers knew the Word of God and were able to test many men who said they were apostles but were lying. The believers also hated the work of the Nicolaitans and the Lord did too, v.6.

These things were very good, but the believers did not love the Lord as much as they had done at first, v.4. He advised them to remember, to turn back to Him, to work for Him and to show that they really loved Him.

We have seen that most Christians in the time of John had lost their first love for the Lord, Frame 260. They were like the church of Ephesus: they knew the Scriptures and could test false teachers, 1 Corinthians 1.5; 1 John 4.1. This was very good and we should do the same; but the Lord also wants us to love Him.

How were the early believers like the church of Ephesus? Pick out the statements which are true.

1. They knew the Scripture and could decide who were false apostles.   FRAME 256

2. Many early Christians died for the Lord's sake.
                                                     FRAME 265

3. Paul had been to Ephesus and told the believers to follow him.   FRAME 269

4. The early believers lost their first love for the Lord Jesus.   FRAME 272

264   No, many churches went through a terrible time of suffering after John had died. For over 200 years the whole Church was like the church of Smyrna. Read Frame 268, the second part, then look again for the correct answer.

265   This is true, but not as many as in the next period. Statement 2 would make the early believers more like the church of Smyrna. Read Frame 263 again and try to find the right answer.

266   The early Church did have a lot of trouble, but it was worse still later on. Read the second paragraph of Frame 260, then try again.

267   The believers in Ephesus rejected false apostles and hated the works of the Nicolaitans. False Jews said evil things against the believers at Smyrna. But in Pergamum the people **accepted** these false teachers and allowed them to stay. This shows that the whole church was getting away from the Lord. Read the first paragraph of Frame 273 and look again for the right answer.

268   The second letter was sent to the church of Smyrna. Read Revelation 2.8-11. This is the shortest of the seven letters. The church of Smyrna had seen a lot of trouble but more was coming. People thought the believers were poor because they did not have many things in the world, but Christ said they were rich because they had a great reward in heaven. Some false teachers said they were Jews but they really belonged to Satan. Many believers were killed, but the Lord promised to give each one a crown of life.

Many believers suffered terrible things while the apostles were still alive. For example, Stephen was killed, Acts 7, and Paul was put in prison for many years. But after John died some of the Roman emperors tried to burn all Bibles and kill all Christians. This happened many times during a period of 200 years.

There are some churches today which the rulers would like to destroy. The believers should remember the Lord's promises in verses 10 and 11. But in early times many thousands of believers were willing to give up their lives for the Lord Jesus. In those days the whole Church on earth was suffering like Smyrna.

Which of these statements is true?

1. The believers of Smyrna suffered more than any other church since the time of John. FRAME 264

2. The church of Smyrna is a picture of the whole Church which suffered terribly for about 200 years after all the apostles had died. FRAME 271

3. It is sometimes better to act as if you did not belong to Christ when people are trying to kill all the Christians. Then you will live longer and be able to serve the Lord. FRAME 277

269   This is true, but the verses in Revelation 2.1-7 do not say anything about Paul. Read these verses and read Frame 263 again and look for a better answer.

270   This is true. Go on to Frame 283.

271   You are right; go to Frame 273.

272   This is true. Did you find another correct statement after Frame 263? If you did, you can go on to Frame 268.

273   The third letter was to the church of Pergamum and it speaks about the third period of the Church Age. Read Revelation 2.12-17. These believers lived where Satan had his throne, but they were true to Christ. The Lord said this was good, but He did not approve of other things. Some of the people of Smyrna followed the teaching of Balaam, a wicked prophet who led the people of Israel into sin. He did this just so King Balak would pay him some money, Numbers 31.16. Other people in Pergamum followed the false teaching of the Nicolaitans, and the Lord told them they must turn from their sins.

We have seen that the churches went through a time of terrible trouble, but this stopped suddenly. A great Roman Emperor, Constantine, made a law which declared that Christians could live like other people. In fact, the Church became quite popular and many people of the world said they were Christians so they could join the Church. The believers in Pergamum lived where Satan's throne was and he is the ruler of this world, Luke 4.6; John 12.31. For many hundreds of years the Church was friendly with the world. The believers accepted false teachers who said that sin was not very bad. This period of the Church Age was like the church of Pergamum.

Which of these statements is true?

1.   There were false teachers in Ephesus and Smyrna and Pergamum, so Pergamum was about the same as the other churches.   FRAME 267

2.   After many long years of trouble the churches were spiritually strong and they rejected at once all false teaching.   FRAME 276

3.   The third period of the Church Age was like the church of Pergamum because the believers lived in the world and began to allow false teachers to remain among them.
                                        FRAME 280

274   It is true that the fourth period of the Church Age was like Thyatira and the Church of Rome was very powerful. But the Lord told the remnant in Thyatira to hold on *until He comes,* so we see that the conditions of Thyatira will continue until the end. Read the second paragraph of Frame 283 and look again for the right answer.

275   They did accept false teaching and this shows that they did not know the Bible. The priests said the Bible was too hard for ordinary people to understand. Read the last paragraph of Frame 278 and try again for the right answer.

276   Trouble and difficulty should make believers strong, but when the churches became popular they allowed false teachers and the Lord did not approve. Read Frame 273 and look for a better answer.

277   No, it is better to tell the truth and confess you belong to Christ. Those who are faithful unto death will receive a crown of life. Read verse 10 and look again for the right answer.

278   We now come to the fourth church, Thyatira. Read Revelation 2.18-29. We have seen that Pergamum was spiritually worse than Ephesus, but Thyatira was worse still.

This church had faith and love and many works, v.19, and the Lord approved what He saw. But the people allowed a woman to teach them that they could commit sin. *Jezebel* was a wicked queen who ruled in Israel, 1 Kings 18-21. The Lord used the same name for this woman in Thyatira. Jezebel was worse than Balaam, and Thyatira was worse than Pergamum. In Pergamum they had people who followed the teaching of Balaam, but in Thyatira this woman taught openly that sin was not really so bad.

The church in the fourth period was much like Thyatira. For hundreds of years the Church of Rome was very strong. The people did not read the Bible and they accepted false teaching. They did many good things and thought they would be saved by their good works. The priests let them sin by telling them the Church would forgive them if they paid money. This was as bad as Jezebel's teaching.

Which of these statements is correct?

1.   In the fourth period of the Church Age the Church of Rome became very powerful and taught the people that their sins would be forgiven if they gave money to the Church.   FRAME 270

2. In the Thyatira period the people knew the Bible well and refused to accept any wrong teaching. FRAME 275

3. In every period the Church became spiritually stronger and better than before.   FRAME 281

279   True; go to Frame 288.

280   True; go to Frame 278.

281   No, we see a decline from Ephesus to Pergamum to Thyatira as the churches began to accept more false teaching. Read Frame 278 again and pick out the true statement.

282   Not at all. No one gets eternal life because he is baptized or is a member of any church. The Lord taught that most of the people in Sardis were spiritually dead and had never received God's gift of life. Read Revelation 3.1 and Frame 288 again. Then you will be able to see the right answer.

283   There were some believers in Thyatira who did not follow the teaching of the wicked Jezebel. The Lord said He would not put any other burden on them, but they should hold what truth they had until He comes again, vs.24,25. A **remnant** is a small number of believers who live in a larger group of people who do not really believe. We can say there was a **remnant** in Thyatira.

We see also that the conditions of Thyatira will continue until the end of the Church Age. The Church of Rome is like Thyatira and it will continue very strong until Christ comes back again. But there are many true believers in the Church of Rome and they really love the Lord. The Son of God promised great rewards to those who win the victory, vs.26-28.

Which of these statements is true?

1. Thyatira could not be a picture of the Church of Rome because the fourth period is past but Rome is still very strong in the world today.   FRAME 274

2. Thyatira is a picture of Rome and it will continue until

the end of the Age, but there is a remnant of believers in the Church of Rome who really love the Lord.

FRAME 279

3.   The Church of Rome forced everybody to follow their teaching so the Lord did not blame the people.

FRAME 286

284   No. The Lord did not say there was anything wrong in Smyrna or Philadelphia and He did not tell the people of these churches to repent. Read the second paragraph of Frame 292 and the verses listed there. Then look for the right answer.

285   No, the Lord promised believers in Philadelphia that He would come soon and the conditions of this church will continue to the end of the Church Age. Read Frame 296 again and you will find the right answer.

286   The Lord will judge all false teachers but we will have to give an account to Him if we follow wrong teaching. He told the remnant to hold what they had and not to give up any more truth. Read Revelation 2.25 and the first paragraph of Frame 283. This will help you to find the right answer.

287   Individuals in the Roman Catholic and Protestant churches may indeed be saved, but the letters to Thyatira and Sardis show that these conditions will continue to the end of the Church Age. In both letters the Lord spoke about His return, 2.25; 3.3. Read Frame 296 and try again.

288   The next church is Sardis; read Revelation 3.1-6. What was happening in Sardis? The people in the church of Sardis thought they had eternal life, but this was not true, v.1. The Lord said their works were not perfect and He would come suddenly when they were not waiting for Him, vs.2,3. However, there were a few who were clean and they would walk with the Lord, v.4.

The fifth period of the Church Age was the time of the Protestant churches. Things became so bad in the Church of Rome that many Christians left and started other churches. They believed that we can be saved by faith alone, and at first most Protestants were true believers who had been born again. But soon many others joined the Protestant churches and today most Protestants do not have eternal life at all.

Still there was a remnant in Sardis and the Lord gave them wonderful promises, vs.4,5. Sardis also will continue to the end of the Church Age, but most Protestants do not expect the Lord to come, so His coming will be **sudden** for them, v.3.

When you have read this Frame carefully, consider the following statements:

1.   All members of Protestant churches have eternal life, if they have been properly baptized.   FRAME 282

2.   The Protestants today are divided into hundreds of denominations and the Roman Catholic Church is far bigger than all of them together. It would be good if all churches would come together and form one big church.   FRAME 289

3.   The church of Sardis stands for the Protestant churches and this period also goes on to the end of the Church Age.   FRAME 293

289   If the churches came together, would the people be taught the truth of God? We have seen that the Roman Catholic and Protestant churches will continue until Christ comes and after that they will all get together. We will take up this subject later on. You should read Frame 288 carefully and you will find the right answer.

290   No. In Thyatira the people followed false teaching, 2.20, and in Sardis they were spiritually dead, 3.1. Read about Philadelphia in Revelation 3.7-13, and read Frame 292 again. This will help you to know the right answer.

291   What verse in the Bible teaches this? The seventh church is Laodicea, and very few people there even wanted the blessing of the Lord. Read all of Frame 299 again and find the right statement or statements.

292   Now read the letter to Philadelphia in Revelation 3.7-13. The Lord found that the believers there had a little power and He opened the door for them to serve Him, v.8. They kept His Word and He promised to keep them from the time of great trouble.

We have seen that there was a remnant in Thyatira and Sardis, a small group of those who loved the Lord when most of the people followed false teaching or were spiritually dead. Now we come to the church of Philadelphia and nothing is said about a remnant. In fact, the church of Philadelphia is itself a remnant of true believers and the Lord did not see anything bad in it. He had to tell all the other churches except Smyrna that they should repent and turn from their sins, 2.5,16,22; 3.3,19.

Which of these sentences is true?

1.   The Lord saw something wrong in all the churches and told them to repent.   FRAME 284

2.   Most of the people in Philadelphia followed false teachings or were spiritually dead.   FRAME 290

3.   The church of Philadelphia was itself a remnant of true believers who had a little power and kept the Lord's Word.   FRAME 295

293   True. Now go to Frame 292.

294   1. Thyatira, Frame 278; 2. Laodicea, Frame 299; 3. Smyrna, Frame 268; 4. Ephesus, Frame 263; 5. Pergamum, Frame 273; 6. Sardis, Frame 288; 7. Philadelphia, Frame 292.

When the Lord comes He will find conditions like those in Thyatira, Sardis, Philadelphia and Laodicea. If you made a mistake read again the Frame number given. When you understand these answers go on to Frame 302.

295   This is correct, but go now to Frame 296 and read about the sixth period of the Church Age.

296   We have seen that conditions like those in Thyatira and Sardis will continue until the end of the Church Age. The

Lord promised the believers in Philadelphia that He would come quickly or soon, v.11, so we know that Philadelphia also will continue until He comes.

When did the Philadelphia period begin? We have seen that the Protestant churches started out well and taught that men can be saved only by faith, but soon the Lord had to say they were spiritually dead. Many true believers left the great Protestant churches and tried to follow the Lord's teaching and to serve Him. So the church of Philadelphia is a picture of the sixth period of the Church Age and it will continue to the end.

Read these statements and decide which is correct.

1.   The church of Philadelphia will be taken over by the great Roman Catholic and Protestant churches.

    FRAME 285

2.   God is blessing the church of Philadelphia today and we can expect that the Roman Catholic and Protestant churches also will come back to the Lord.   FRAME 287

3.   The Philadelphia period started when many true believers left the Protestant churches because these churches had given up the truth. There will be many churches like Philadelphia right to the end of the Church Age.   FRAME 298

297   This is true, but before you go on check the other statements after Frame 299 to see if either of them is true.

298   True. Go to Frame 299.

299   The last message is to the church of Laodicea; read Revelation 3.14-22. The people in Laodicea had not fully rejected the Word of God, but they did not love the Lord. They were not cold but they were not really hot either. The Lord was ready to put them away completely, vs.15,16. They thought they were rich but the Lord told them they were very poor, vs.17,18. Still He loved them and promised to enter the heart of anyone who would let Him in, vs.19,20.

This is the general condition of many churches in the world

today. We are in the last period of the Church Age. Many believers are rich and have everything the world can sell them. They do not turn right away from Christ nor follow false teachers. But they do not love the Lord enough to leave everything and go out and serve Him.

Which of these three statements is or are true?

1. The churches will have a great time of blessing before the Lord comes.   FRAME 291

2. The church of Laodicea was neither cold nor hot and many churches today are just like it.   FRAME 297

3. People thought the believers in Smyrna were poor but the Lord said they were rich. People in Laodicea thought they were rich but the Lord said they were poor.   FRAME 301

300   So we see that the seven churches of Asia stand for seven periods of the Church Age. The Lord saw what was good and what was wrong in each church and each period. He saw nothing wrong in two churches, but the others seem to get worse and worse.

Four of the seven periods go right on to the end and we can see these conditions in the world today. Many people are in the Roman Catholic Church and they follow false teachers. Others are in one of the Protestant churches; they should know the truth but they are spiritually dead. A few love the Lord and He gives them opportunity to serve Him, but most people seem to be rich in money but really they are very poor in spiritual treasure.

Some people feel badly because they belong to some church which is like Thyatira or Sardis or Laodicea and think that they cannot do anything about it. Read the Lord's promises to each *remnant*, 2.24,25; 3.4,20. There are also promises in every letter to those who win the victory. At the end of the Church Age, the Lord knows those who love Him and keep His Word. They are truly in the church of Philadelphia and the Lord will keep all believers from the time of great trouble which is coming soon.

Write in the name of the church which is best described by each statement.

1. The people follow false teachers _____

2. They are neither cold nor hot _____

3. They would soon pass through more trouble _____

4. They left their first love _____

5. They lived where Satan's throne is _____

6. They should know the truth but are spiritually dead.

_____

7. They have a little strength and have not denied His name.

_____

Now put a mark beside the names of the churches which will be here in the world when the Lord comes. Look at Frame 294 to check your answers.

301   Your answer is correct and so there are two true statements after Frame 299. Now consider this question: Which is more important, what men think or what the Lord thinks? It is better to be poor in this world and to have riches in heaven. We can save up treasure in heaven by serving the Lord Jesus Christ, Matthew 6.20. If you understand these things, go to Frame 300.

302   Now look at Chart 6. We can add more details to Chart 5 because we now know something about the Church Age. The Church Age started when the Holy Spirit came down on the on the day of Pentecost and it will last until the Rapture. There are seven periods in the Church Age, some much longer than others. Each of these periods has conditions like those in one of the seven churches.

Chart 6

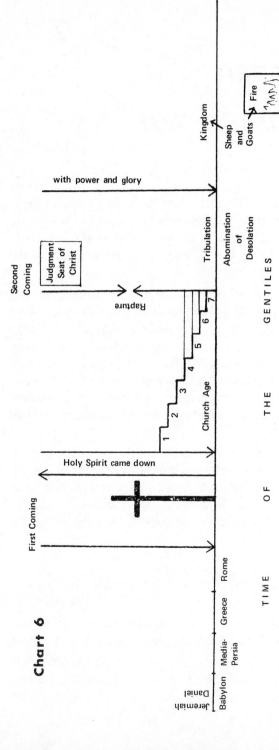

Most of the time the Church was going down spiritually but the Lord saw nothing wrong in Smyrna or Philadelphia. The last four churches continue until the end of the Age. Then the Lord will take up to heaven all the true Christians in the world. The dead churches will not be destroyed at once; we will consider what will happen to these churches in Lesson 11.

Study Chart 6 and try to understand everything on it. Then go to Lesson 7 and Frame 303.

7

AFTER

THE CHURCH AGE

303 The Church Age will be over when the Lord comes, and the Church will go to be with Him at the Rapture. What will happen after the Rapture? We have already seen that the Lord will give rewards and crowns to His people at the Judgment Seat of Christ, Frames 84, 87 and 230.

Some believers may be very sad at the Judgment Seat of Christ, those who see that their lives on earth were wasted, 1 Corinthians 3.15. But after that there will be a time of great joy, like a wedding feast. We have seen that the Church is like the Bride of Christ, Frame 238. In Revelation the Lord Jesus is called the *Lamb* 28 times. Men killed Him but He will receive great honour and glory, 5.12. Christ is the most important Person at the wedding feast and so it is called the wedding feast of the Lamb. Read Revelation 19.5-9.

The Church will be there as the Lamb's Bride, dressed in beautiful white linen. Other believers will be invited to be there: they were saved before the Church Age, so they are not members of Christ's Body, John 3.29. Best of all, the Lamb of God, the Lord Jesus Christ, will be there and will receive honour and glory from everyone.

Which is true?

1. Some believers will be sad at the wedding feast of the Lamb.   FRAME 306

2. The wedding feast of the Lamb will come after the Judgment Seat of Christ and the Church will be there as the Bride of Christ.   FRAME 310

3. In the joy of heaven the Lord will forget all about the time when men killed Him.   FRAME 312

304   Surely you have learned that there will be a time of great tribulation which will last until the Lord comes. Read Frame 182 and Frame 308 again and find the right answer.

305   This is true. Go to Frame 318.

306   Many will be sad at the Judgment Seat of Christ, but when it is over we will all be happy with the Lord. Read Revelation 19.7-9 and the first part of Frame 303 again, then try for the right answer.

307   Two leaders will not be killed, but they will not escape: they will be thrown into the lake of fire. Read verse 20 and Frame 318 again and look for the right answer.

308   The wedding feast of the Lamb will take place in heaven. What will be happening on earth at that time? We have seen that the Lord will return to earth and rule as King, but before that there will be a time of great tribulation. In Matthew 24 we read about the beginning of Pain, the Great Tribulation, and the coming of the Son of Man, Frame 182. Men will hate God's people and try to destroy them. The Jews will have to run away, Matthew 24.16-20. A Gentile king called the little horn will fight against the people of God until the Lord comes, Daniel 7.21,22.

In Revelation 19 we learn that the Lord will come and suddenly destroy His enemies and those who are trying to kill all God's people.

Read these statements carefully and decide which one is true.

1.   When the Lord comes He will find peace in the world and all people living safely and quietly together.
                                                        FRAME 304

2.   The little horn will welcome the Lord Jesus when He comes to rule as King of kings.   FRAME 311

3.   Before the Lord comes, His enemies will try to destroy His people on earth and there will be Great Tribulation.
                                                        FRAME 314

309   Oh no, the Son of God has a sword, v.15, and He will defeat the nations instantly. Read Revelation 19.19,20. There is no period of time which must pass before the leaders are taken as prisoners. Read Frame 313 again and you will be able to find the right answer.

310   This is true. You may go to Frame 308.

311   No. The little horn will attack God's people and the Lord will come to save them. Look again for the right answer.

312   The Lord will not be sad in heaven, but He will always have the scars of the nails in His hands. In Revelation He is often called the Lamb, and this name speaks of His death. Read Revelation 7.14 and 13.8; also Frame 303 again. This will help you to find the right answer.

313   Read Revelation 19.11-16. Here we see a wonderful picture of our Lord Jesus Christ riding on a white horse. He has four names: 1. Faithful and True, v.11
2. A name which only He can know, v.12
3. The Word of God, v.13
4. King of kings and Lord of lords, v.16

He will come to judge the world, save His people and destroy their enemies. First an angel will call all the birds to come and eat the flesh of those who hate God, vs.17,18. The kings of earth will gather their armies to fight against the Son of God, v.19. Of course the battle will not last long. The leaders will be taken as prisoners and their armies destroyed, vs.20,21.

Consider and choose:

1.   Christ will come in power and glory and will destroy all those who hate God.   FRAME 305

2.   All men will join together to fight against Christ and it will take years for the Lord to win the war against them.
          FRAME 309

3.   Men would never be foolish enough to suppose they could fight against God.   FRAME 317

314   True. You may now go to Frame 313.

315   This is true, but see if you can find another true statement after Frame 318.

316   No, Satan will not be able to deceive men or tempt them to sin against God. Read verse 3 and the last part of Frame 323 and try again.

317   Men should know better than to fight against God because God is stronger than all His creatures together. Read Psalm 2.1-6 and you will see the people of the world trying to fight against God and Christ. Also read Revelation 19.19 and find the true statement after Frame 313.

318   The Son of God will be able to destroy His enemies, but two men will be captured alive. These two men are called the *beast* and the *false prophet,* Revelation 19.19,20. Who are these men? Remember that Daniel saw four wild animals in a dream and they were pictures of four great kings, Daniel 7.17. Here the beast will be a king, the leader of the kings of the world when they go to fight against the Son of God, v.19.

The Lord Jesus said there will be many false messiahs and prophets who will perform great miracles just before He comes, Matthew 24.24. One of these false prophets will help the beast by telling people to worship him. We will learn more about the beast and the False Prophet when we read Revelation 13 and Lesson 9. Here we see that these two wicked men will be thrown alive into the lake of fire, v.20.

Which of these statements is or are true?

1. The Man on the white horse will destroy all His enemies, but two of the leaders will escape.   FRAME 307

2. Christ will capture the beast and the False Prophet alive and throw them into the lake of fire.   FRAME 315

3. There will be two great leaders in the future; the political leader will rule over the kings and the religious leader will make people worship a man.   FRAME 322

319   True, God will not force people to believe the Bible, but Satan **did** tempt Eve to disobey God's command. Read 2 Corinthians 11.3 and remember, the Bible is true. You will find the right answer if you read Frame 323 again more carefully.

320   No, they will have a part in the first Resurrection and will rule with Christ for a thousand years. Read Revelation 20.4-6 and Frame 327 again.

321   True, but you should look at the statements after Frame 334 again and find another true statement.

322   This is true. Did you find another true statement after Frame 318? If you understand them both, go to Frame 323.

323   So two great enemies will be put away. We now come to men's greatest enemy and see that he will be tied up for a thousand years. Read Revelation 20.1-3. This enemy has four names: 1. *Dragon.* This fierce animal is a picture of Satan in Revelation.

2. *That old serpent.* Satan came as a snake and tempted Eve, Genesis 3.1.

3. *Devil.* This word means that Satan *accuses* the people of God, Revelation 12.10.

4. *Satan.* This name means that he is always the *enemy* of God and His people, 1 Thessalonians 2.18.

Here we see that the angel will tie the dragon with a chain and throw him into a great hole. Satan will not be able to deceive men for a thousand years. The Lord Jesus Christ will rule over the whole world for this period of time, which is called the Millennium. We will read more about the Millennium in the next Lesson.

Consider these three statements. Which one is true?

1.   Satan will be tied up for a thousand years but will continue to deceive men while he is in prison.   FRAME 316

2.   People don't have to believe these old stories about the snake talking to a woman and telling her to eat an apple.
FRAME 319

3.   Christ will rule for a thousand years and Satan will not
       be able to tempt God's people during those years.

FRAME 326

324   No, all men will rise from death, some will have eternal
           life, some will rise and stand before God's judgment throne.
Read John 5.28,29; this will help you to understand. Then look
for the right answer.

325   True, but there are two true statements, so you must find
           both. Then go to Frame 337.

326   This is correct. Go to Frame 327.

327   Christ the King of kings will rule over the world for a thou-
           sand years and His people will rule with Him. You can read
about some of these people in Revelation 20.4-6. In the time of
Great Tribulation many believers will be killed because they speak
about Christ and will not follow the beast. They will rise from
death when Christ comes and rule with Him for a thousand years.

We have seen that all believers will rise from death when the
Lord comes at the time of the Rapture. This is the first Resurrection. Many Jews will turn to the Lord during the Tribulation
and will go and preach the Good News to the Gentiles, Matthew
24.14. Some of these believers will be killed, both Jews and Gentiles. They will have a part in the first Resurrection and rise from
death when Christ comes in power and glory. (Wicked men will
also rise from death, but not until after the Millennium, as we shall
see in Frame 337.)

Which of these statements is or are true?

1.   Believers who die after the Rapture will rise from death
      after the Millennium.   FRAME 320

2.   All believers will rise again to life, but when sinners die
      they are dead forever.   FRAME 324

3.   After the Rapture many believers will be killed for
      Christ's sake, but they will rise from death when He
      comes in power and glory.   FRAME 330

328   No, never think anyone can escape from God's judgment by having his body burned. God is able to raise everyone from death and will certainly judge all men who have rejected Christ. Read Hebrews 9.27 and Frame 337 again.

329   All right; now go to Frame 341.

330   You are right; go to Frame 334.

331   Satan knew quite well what he was doing when he first sinned against God and God will never give him a chance to repent. Eve was deceived when she sinned and so God gives men the opportunity to repent. Satan will be set loose from prison but will at once start to fight against God again. Read verses 7 and 8 and Frame 334 again.

332   Many people talk about a general Judgment, but the Bible says only the wicked will stand before the Great White Throne and all of them will have to go to the lake of fire. Read John 5.24 and the last paragraph of Frame 337 again.

333   All men **must** bow before Christ; His enemies will hate to do this but will be forced to obey. Read Romans 14.11, Philippians 2.10 and Frame 341 again.

334   Everything will be wonderful when the Lord Jesus rules on earth for a thousand years. We will learn more about the Millennium in Lesson 8, but here in Revelation 20.7-10 we read about the end of this period.

After a thousand years Satan will be set free and will at once start again to deceive people. He will persuade men to fight against God by fighting against His people and by trying to capture Jerusalem. But God will judge them quickly and destroy them with fire from heaven. Then Satan will be thrown into the lake of fire and tormented forever.

Read carefully these three statements and decide which is or are true.

1. After the Millennium Satan will again try to fight against God, but he will be thrown into the lake of fire.
    FRAME 321

2. The beast will try to fight against Christ, but the Lord will destroy his followers with His sword. A thousand years later Satan will try to take the city of Jerusalem, but his followers will be destroyed by fire. FRAME 325

3. After a thousand years in prison Satan will repent and obey God from then on and forever.   FRAME 331

335   True. Go to Frame 348.

336   True. You may go to Frame 345.

337   All men will rise from death, 1 Corinthians 15.21,22. Believers will rise at the first resurrection, Frame 327.

All other men will rise at the second resurrection and stand before God to be judged. Revelation 20.12-15 tells us about the Great White Throne.

1. No one will be able to escape, because the earth and heaven will disappear, v.11, and there will be no place to go.

2. All wicked people will be there, both great and small, v.12.

3. No one will be able to say he never committed sin because the books will show what everyone has done, v.12.

Another book will show the names of all who have eternal life. All believers will be raised a thousand years before this, but all wicked people will be thrown into the lake of fire at this time.

Which of these sentences is true?

1. Many people ask that their bodies should be burned after they die. This is the best way to escape from God's judgment.   FRAME 328

2. All wicked people will rise from death, stand before the Great White Throne and then go to the lake of fire.
    FRAME 329

3. At the Great White Throne God will decide who can go into heaven and who must go to the lake of fire.
    FRAME 332

338   This is true. Go to Frame 351.

339   No, God's servants will be very happy because they will
be able to serve Him. Read Revelation 5.8-14; 22.3. Those
with harps will sing praise to God. There will be only joy in heaven,
no joy outside of heaven. Read again the seven things we will find
in heaven and try for the right answer.

340   No, this world will be burned with fire and will vanish
away. God created the first earth and He can surely create
another. Read 2 Peter 3.10,12; Revelation 20.11, and Frame 345.

341   John saw the Person who will sit on the Great White Throne
and judge all men who will stand before Him. He is called
God, v.12, and from John 5.22,23,27, we learn that it is the Son
of God, the Lord Jesus Christ, who is also the Son of Man.

Men will be judged by the God-Man. As God He knows everything men have ever done. He also has the power to punish them
and He will always do what is right.

As Son of Man He knows that men are weak and He knows
how they feel. The Son of Man died for the sins of all men and He
will judge those who have refused Him. Many people reject Christ
today; they will certainly fall on their knees before Him later,
Philippians 2.10.

Choose the true statement:

1.   Some people reject Christ today and will never bow
before Him.   FRAME 333

2.   Christ, the God-Man, is the One who will judge men.
                                                FRAME 336

3.   Jesus taught us to love our enemies and at the end He
will forgive everybody.   FRAME 343

342   No. Only righteousness and righteous people will live in
the new world and no enemy will be allowed in it. Read
1 Corinthians 15.25-28 and 2 Peter 3.13, and the last paragraph
of Frame 345.

343   Not so. Christ offers His mercy to all men, but will never force anyone to accept it. Absalom never asked his father David to forgive him for killing his brother. David brought him back to the city and kissed him, but Absalom soon tried to kill his father David, 2 Samuel 14.33; 17.2,4. God has given men every opportunity; many will not repent now and they will not be able to do so later. Read Revelation 20.15 and the last paragraph of Frame 341.

344   The Roman Catholic Church teaches this, but the Bible does not. In one old book, people are told they should pray for those who have died. This book might make you think believers have to suffer for their sins and today some Bibles include this book. But the true Word of God is found in 66 books of the Bible which never say believers suffer after death, nor that we should pray for them. Read Frame 351 again.

345   What will happen after all wicked men have been thrown into the lake of fire with Satan? God will then destroy heaven and earth and create a new heaven and new earth. Men's sin has brought a curse on this earth and wicked spirits live in the heavenly world, Genesis 3.17; Ephesians 6.12. God will destroy heaven and earth with fire and create a new heaven and earth which will continue forever, 2 Peter 3.10; Isaiah 65.17; 66.22.

In Revelation 21.1 we read that John saw a new heaven and a new earth. Peter tells us that there will be no sin or evil in the new earth; only righteousness and righteous people will live in it, 2 Peter 3.13. We will see in Lesson 8 that the new earth will be better than this earth during the Millennium, Frame 407.

Read and choose the true statement.

1.   God will destroy this earth and create a new heaven and earth.   FRAME 335

2.   In the future everything will be perfect on this earth and God will call it His new earth.   FRAME 340

3.   Even in the new earth some men will fall into sin and God will have to punish them.   FRAME 342

346   The proper order of events will be: The Wedding Feast.
Christ will come in power and glory; the First Resurrection
(second part); the Millennium; the Great White Throne; the new
heaven and earth. Go to Frame 359.

347   No, wicked men will suffer in the lake of fire forever with
the beast and the False Prophet. They will never be able to
escape. They will never have another chance to repent. We ought
to tell them **now** how to be saved. Read the second part of Frame
351 again.

348   What will heaven be like? In Revelation 21.1 to 22.5 we
read about heaven and the new Jerusalem. Notice seven
things which will **not** be in heaven:

1. No sorrow or pain, 21.4.
2. No temple, because God Himself will be there, 21.22.
3. No sun or moon, because God will give light, 21.23.
4. No night, 21.25 and 22.5.
5. No evil thing or wicked man, 21.27.
6. No curse, 22.3.
7. No hunger or thirst, 7.16.

    We **will** find these things in heaven:

1. Light, 21.23.
2. Life, people whose names are in the Lamb's book
   of life, 21.27.
3. The river of life, 22.1.
4. The tree of life, 22.2.
5. The throne of God and the Lamb, 22.3.
6. God's servants will worship Him and see His face, 22.3,4.
7. His name will be on their foreheads, 22.4.

    Look up these verses and, when you understand, consider
these sentences and decide which is true.

1.   Nothing bad will be in heaven and the Lamb will give
      us everything we need.   FRAME 338

2.   In heaven there is nothing to do except to play on
      harps all the time.   FRAME 339

3.   In the end everybody will be in heaven.   FRAME 350

349   The Bible speaks about going *up* to heaven, Romans 10.6, but it does not tell us where heaven is. Who will *be in heaven* is more important than *where heaven is.* Read the first part of Frame 353 again.

350   Not so. This is Satan's lie to keep people from believing in Christ. No one will be in heaven unless his name is in the Lamb's book of the living. Read Revelation 21.27 and look again for the true statement.

351   What about hell and the lake of fire? The word hell sometimes means the place where people go when they die; sometimes it means the place of fire. In Revelation we read about the lake of fire.

1. The beast and the False Prophet must go there, 19.20.
2. The devil must go there, 20.10.
3. All wicked men must go there, 20.15; 21.8.

No believer will ever go to the lake of fire, 2.11; 20.6, and no one there will ever escape from it, 20.10. The lake of fire is called the second death, 20.14; 21.8, and the people there will be very sad and also angry against God, Matthew 13.42.

Which is true?

1.   Many believers will go to a place of fire to make them pure enough to enter heaven.   FRAME 344

2.   After a thousand years God will let all men out of the lake of fire, but Satan and his angels will stay there forever.   FRAME 347

3.   Satan will be thrown into the lake of fire, also the beast and the False Prophet and all wicked men. There they will be sad and angry against God forever.   FRAME 354

352   Words cannot fully describe the place where wicked men will suffer forever. It will be worse than a lake of fire or a terribly dark place. Make sure that you believe the Bible and trust in the Lord Jesus Christ. Read all of Frame 353 again and look for the true statement.

353   Where are heaven and hell? Some people think that heaven
is up in the sky and the lake of fire is down in the earth.
The Bible does not tell us where heaven and the lake of fire are but
we know that heaven is where the Lord Jesus is. He asked the
Father that we should be with Him where He is, John 17.24. This
is the important thing about heaven.

All wicked men will go to a place called the lake of fire. It is
a place of terrible darkness, 2 Peter 2.17; Jude 13. Worst of all, it
is far away from God. The wicked will be separated from the
Lord forever because they did not believe the Gospel, 2 Thessalonians 1.8,9. We ought to warn them to believe in Christ before it
is too late.

We have been looking forward into the future. What do we
see in the Bible?

1.   Heaven is up in the sky in a part of space where there
      are no stars.   FRAME 349

2.   The Bible says that wicked men will go to a dark place
      called the lake of fire, but there is no such place because
      fire is not dark.   FRAME 352

3.   We do not know where heaven is, but we will be there
      with the Lord Jesus, and this is the most important
      thing.   FRAME 356

354   True. Now you may go to Frame 353.

355   How long will the new heaven and earth continue to exist?
We will answer this question by asking two others: How
long will God exist? How long will His servants live?

1. God will live forever, Revelation 15.7.

2. God's servants will rule as kings forever, Revelation 22.5.

How long is *forever?* Think of the two biggest numbers you
know. Multiply them together. Forever is much longer than the
biggest number of years we can think about. There will be about
7,000 years between the time of Adam and the end of the Millennium, but God existed in eternity long before He created Adam.
After the Millennium we will be in the eternity of the future. The
7,000 years are like a small stone between two great mountains.

Eternity is much greater than the time men have been on the earth. There will be no end to the new heaven and the new earth.

We must also say that there will be no end to the lake of fire. Read Revelation 14.11; 19.3; 20.10. Ask the Lord to help you warn your friends not to wait any longer.

Which are true?

1.   Heaven will last as long as God exists, which is forever.
                                                          FRAME 358

2.   The lake of fire will last as long as God exists, which is forever.   FRAME 358

3.   God's servants will live as long as God exists, which is forever.   FRAME 358

356   Correct. You may go to Frame 355.

357   We have been studying Revelation 19.1 to 21.5. Think of these six great events and write down beside number 1 at the right which event will come first. Then write beside number 2 the second event, and all the others in proper order down to the last one.

The Lord will come in power and glory.   1. _____

The First Resurrection (second part)   2. _____

The Great White Throne   3. _____

The Millennium   4. _____

The new heaven and earth   5. _____

The Wedding Feast   6. _____

Think carefully about your answers, then turn to Frame 346 to see if you got them all right.

358   All three statements are true. When you understand Frame 355 go to Frame 357.

Chart 7

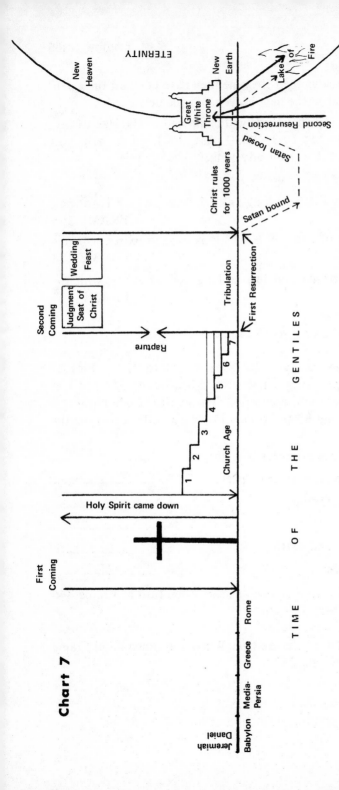

359 Now look carefully at Chart 7. We are able to add several important events which we have learned about in Lesson 7. Notice these words on Chart 7:

Satan will be tied up for 1,000 years.

The First Resurrection

The Great White Throne

The New Heaven and Earth

Eternity

Be sure you understand these very important things before you go on to Frame 360 in Lesson 8.

8

ONE THOUSAND

WONDERFUL YEARS

360   God gave His people many promises which we can read in
the Old Testament. Some of these promises have already
been fulfilled and therefore we can be sure that God will do
everything that He has promised.

God's servants wrote down many promises about Christ.
Some of these tell about the time when Christ first came to earth.
For example:

God told Micah that the Ruler of Israel would be born in
Bethlehem; Christ was born there, Micah 5.2; Matthew 2.6.

God told David that his son or descendant would be King
forever; Christ was David's Descendant, 2 Samuel 7.12,13,16;
Matthew 22.42; Romans 1.3.

God told Isaiah that Christ's mother would be a virgin; we
know that the Holy Spirit came on Mary before she was married,
Isaiah 7.14; Matthew 1.20-23.

God fulfilled these promises when Christ came the first time.
He will fulfill many more when Christ comes back again. Some
day all His promises will come to pass.

Now consider which of these statements is true.

1.   A man can talk about the future and if he guesses right,
people say he is a prophet. If he is wrong, they just
forget about it.   FRAME 363

2.   God's prophets said many things about Christ. Some of
these things have already come true, so we can be sure
that God will fulfill the other prophecies also.

FRAME 365

3.   We know the Bible is true because everything God promised through His prophets has been fulfilled.

FRAME 367

361   David and Isaiah did have a lot of trouble but the Holy Spirit led them to write about Christ too. We know this from the New Testament. Read Frame 366 again and note carefully all the New Testament verses given.

362   How could He? He will come for His people and take them to heaven. Later He will bring them back with Him when He comes to rule. Read Frame 370 again and look for the right answer.

363   Not in Israel. God commanded the people of Israel to kill anyone who claimed to be a prophet but did not tell the truth, Deuteronomy 18.20-22. We believe God's prophets were true prophets because God fulfilled what He had promised to them. Therefore we can be sure He will fulfill all His promises. Look at the examples in Frame 360 and ask yourself which statement is true.

364   This is true, but look for another true statement. Is statement 2 true, or statement 3?

365   This is right. Go to Frame 366.

366   God made many promises which were fulfilled when Christ came to earth. For example:

We know Psalm 22 speaks of Christ and His death because He Himself used the words of verse 1 when He was on the cross, Matthew 27.46. God promised not to leave Him in the grave, Psalm 16.10, and He raised Him from death, Acts 2.31; 13.35-37.

We know Isaiah 53 is speaking about Christ because Philip said so, Acts 8.31-35. In Isaiah 53.4,5 we learn that Messiah would come and suffer for our sins. Many verses in the New Testament tell us that this is the reason for Christ's death, for example, 1 Peter 3.18.

There are also many promises in the Old Testament which tell about Christ's **glory**. For example, in Isaiah 32.1 we see that a King will come and rule righteously. These promises were not fulfilled when Christ came the first time, but He will come again with power and glory.

Think and choose:

1. David and Isaiah wrote about their own suffering and trouble and never thought about Christ coming hundreds of years later. FRAME 361

2. The Old Testament prophets said that men would reject Christ and also give Him great glory. These both cannot be true. FRAME 368

3. In the Bible we read that Christ would suffer and also receive glory from men. He suffered when He came the first time and will receive the glory when He returns. FRAME 371

367 Not everything. God has already fulfilled many promises and we are sure that the Bible is true, but God has promised many wonderful things about the future and they will certainly come to pass. Read Frame 360 again and find the right answer.

368 They both could not be true *at the same time* and the prophets did not understand everything they wrote. Now we know that the suffering was at the first coming and the glory will be at the second. Read 1 Peter 1.10 and 11, also read Frame 366 very carefully and you will find the right answer.

369 No, it is better to think of two comings of Christ. The first coming had two parts and the second also will have two parts. Read the last paragraph in Frame 370 again and try for the correct answer.

370 Let us look still more closely at some Old Testament prophecies. First, Micah 5.2 says the ruler of Israel will come from Bethlehem and we know the Lord Jesus was born there, Matthew 2.1. Then Zechariah 9.9 says He would come riding on a donkey and so He did, Matthew 21.4-7.

Both of these Old Testament verses were fulfilled at Christ's first coming. The first one in Micah took place when the Lord was born, the other in Zechariah when He was a Man. We see that there was about 30 years' difference, yet both mean the first coming.

So in the New Testament we read that Christ will come first **for** His people, 1 Thessalonians 4.16. Later He will come **with** His people and the holy angels, 1 Thessalonians 3.13. In Lesson 10 we will see that there will be about seven years between these two parts of the second coming.

When you understand this Frame think about these statements and choose one.

1. Christ will come for His people and with His people at the same time.   FRAME 362

2. There are four different kinds of prophecies and we should say Christ has come twice already and will come twice more.   FRAME 369

3. There were two parts to Christ's first coming and there will be two parts to His second coming.   FRAME 373

371   True. Now go to Frame 370.

372   No, Ezekiel said that God's servant *David* would rule over His people but this really means the Messiah, the Descendant of David. Read Frame 379 again.

373   This is true; you may go to Frame 375.

374   This is true, but go again to Frame 381 and find another true statement.

375   The Old Testament writers did not know about the Church, the Body of Christ. The Holy Spirit gave this great truth to the apostle Paul, Ephesians 3.4-6. The Lord also told Paul first about the Rapture, 1 Thessalonians 4.15. In the Old

Testament we see wonderful promises that Christ will come in power and glory. In the New Testament we learn also that there are two parts to the second coming; the Rapture will take place first.

Read these statements and choose one or two.

1. The **New** Testament teaches us about the Church and the Rapture of the Church.   FRAME 364

2. Paul was the only person in the Bible who wrote about the Rapture and he could have been wrong. FRAME 378

3. Many Old Testament writers show that Christ would come twice.   FRAME 380

376   True, but is there another true statement?

377   This is true, but not the only true statement after Frame 379.

378   No, Paul wrote as the Holy Spirit told him and we should believe everything God says. Paul wrote in 1 Thessalonians 4.15 just what the Lord had taught him. Read Frame 375 again and look for the correct answer.

379   Let us look then at some of God's promises in the Old Testament which say that Christ will come as King of kings.

1. All kings will bow before the Descendant of David, Psalm 72.11.

2. The Branch or Descendant of David will rule in Judah, Jeremiah 23.5; 33.15,21.

3. The Son of Man will rule over all nations, Daniel 7.13,14.

God promised that a descendant of David will rule as King over the whole world. His name is Jesus Christ, Revelation 11.15. When Christ rules, there will be peace for a thousand years.

Which **are** true?

1. David himself will rise from death and rule over Israel and the whole world.   FRAME 372

2. The Messiah was called the Branch of David and the Son of David, but we know His name is the Lord Jesus Christ.   FRAME 377

3. God's prophets said long ago that a future King in David's family will rule over Israel and all nations.
                                                FRAME 382

380   This is also true. You should understand **two** true statements after Frame 375. If you do, go to Frame 379.

381   King David belonged to the tribe of Judah and so did the Lord Jesus Christ. The Lord will rule over Israel and all the nations of the world. Israel will be the leading nation in the Kingdom.

Before the Lord comes the Jews will go through a time of great trouble and many will run away to save their lives. Others will go to distant countries to preach the good news, Matthew 24.14,16.

When the Lord comes He will first send His angels to gather the Jews together, Matthew 24.31. They will live in the land of Israel in peace during the Kingdom Age, Amos 9.14,15.

The Lord will build a temple of God, Zechariah 6.12, 13. God gave Ezekiel a great vision of this temple, Ezekiel 40-48. In the Millennium all people should come to worship the Lord at Jerusalem and God will punish those who do not come, Zechariah 14.17-19.

Think and choose one or two right statements.

1. The new temple at Jerusalem will be the center for all nations to come and worship the Lord.   FRAME 374

2. Many Jews are returning to Israel today and when the Lord comes they will all be there to welcome Him.
                                                FRAME 384

3. The Lord will gather the Jews and make Israel the leading nation in His Kingdom.   FRAME 387

382   This is true, but there is another true statement also. When you understand both go to Frame 381.

383   True, heaven is not on earth and heaven will last forever. See if you can find another statement which also shows that the Kingdom is **different** from heaven.

384   No, most of the Jews will be scattered around the world during the period before Christ comes in power and glory. Read the second paragraph of Frame 381 again and find the right answer.

385   In this world, yes, but in the Kingdom the Lord Jesus will help the poor and force all men to act righteously. Read the last paragraph again and find the correct answer.

386   In the world today many people are unfair to others. Even countries with good laws do not always have honest judges and officers.

Some Christians think that they can improve things in this world, but the Lord Jesus told us to preach the Gospel so men can be saved.

When the Lord comes He will first fight against all God's enemies and of course Christ will get the victory. In Psalm 2 we read about the enemies who rise up against God and Christ. God will give Christ the power to rule on Mount Zion in Jerusalem and to control all nations, Psalm 2.2,3,6,8,9.

In the Kingdom Christ will rule righteously and help all poor people, Isaiah 11.4,5. Wicked men will not get rich as they often do today, Isaiah 32.1,5. All men will have to do that which is right, Isaiah 26.9 (second part).

Read all these verses carefully, then choose one or two of these statements.

1.   Christ will defeat His enemies and rule righteously and fairly in the world.   FRAME 376

2.   In the world some people will always be poor and some will be wicked.   FRAME 385

3.   Many kings will unite to rebel against God, but still He will put His King, His Son, on the Throne. FRAME 390

387   This is true, but there is another true statement at the end of Frame 381. Do you understand them both? If so, go to Frame 386.

388   Many world leaders are afraid that this will come true, but we think that Christ will come before that and if He does He will look after all the needs of all the people. You can find a better answer than this, so try again.

389   True, in heaven no one will be married or have children, but on earth people will have lots of children, Luke 18.16. Find another statement about the difference between the Kingdom and heaven. When you understand these statements turn to Frame 395.

390   True. Did you decide another statement also is true? If you got both right, go to Frame 391.

391   The Kingdom of Christ on earth will be like heaven in one way: only true believers can enter. No one can see the Kingdom of God unless he has the new life, John 3.3. And no sinner can enter heaven unless his name is written in the Book of the living, Revelation 21.27.

There are many differences between heaven and the Kingdom. No one will get married or have a wife in heaven, all people are like the angels, Matthew 22.30. On earth living believers will enter the Kingdom when Christ comes. They will get married and have many children. These children will grow up and get married and have many more children. All these people will have to obey the King who will rule righteously. Some of them will trust in Christ and they will be born again. Everyone will know the Lord, Isaiah 11.9; Jeremiah 31.34, but some will not love Him.

One great difference between heaven and the Kingdom of God on earth is:

    1.   The Kingdom is on earth and it will last for only a thousand years.   FRAME 383

    2.   Believers on earth will have children, but not in heaven.   FRAME 389

3.   Only those who are born again can enter.   FRAME 393

392   All this is true; go right on to Frame 402.

393   This is true, but it shows that the Kingdom is **like** heaven. Look only for the statements which show that the Kingdom is **different** from heaven.

394   Men will work, Isaiah 65.21, 22; Ezekiel 28.26, but everything will be much easier than now. Look again for the right answer after Frame 395.

395   Today many leaders are afraid that there will soon be too many people to feed. In the Kingdom there will be plenty of food for everyone.

1. The ground will produce good crops and deserts will be like gardens, Isaiah 35.1; 51.3; Ezekiel 36.34,35.

2. Wild animals will become tame, Isaiah 11.6-8.

3. Christ will heal people and most men will live to a very old age, Isaiah 65.20; Malachi 4.2.

Which of these statements is true?

1.   The population of the world will double in the next 35 years and millions will be starving.   FRAME 388

2.   In the Kingdom there will be huge crops and so much food that people will not have to work any more.
    FRAME 394

3.   In the Kingdom there will be many millions of healthy people living to a great age, but there will be enough food for all.   FRAME 398

396   This is true, but what about the Millennium? Look again for another answer which tells more about the Millennium or the Kingdom Age.

397   Christ should rule in our hearts, yes, but why would God refuse to send Christ back to earth? Men rejected Christ on the earth and God has glorified Him in heaven. It is important that

Christ will be glorified right here on earth. The Jews will see the Man whom their nation nailed to the cross, Zechariah 12.10. He will rule over the Gentiles, Romans 15.12. Read Frame 402 again and get the right answer.

398   True, go to Frame 399.

399   What else can we learn about the Kingdom?

1. There will be peace all over the world and nations will not have to spend millions just to maintain huge armies. The Lord is called the *Prince of Peace,* Isaiah 9.6.

2. There will be no crime or any need for the police when Christ rules with power and righteousness.

3. False religions demand a great deal of money today but they will not exist in the Kingdom.

You can see that there will be plenty for all people when Christ rules as King over the world.

We can help people today by telling them about Christ. Those who are saved can give their money to the Lord instead of giving it to the wicked priests or teachers of some false religion. The Lord Jesus will give us rewards if we use our money and time to serve Him.

What will the Millennium be like? Pick out one or two true statements.

1.   Three things today take a lot of money which could be used to help people: war, crime, and false religion. Christ will not allow these things when He is King.
                                                                    FRAME 392

2.   Millions are wasted today because world leaders must prepare for war.   FRAME 396

3.   When Jesus is King everybody will love each other and all will be free to worship in their own way. FRAME 401

400   There will be great blessing on this earth in the Millennium but God has a plan for something better still. Read Frame 407 again and find the right answer or answers.

401   Everybody will be free to worship Jehovah, but God will not allow any false religion at all. Look again for the correct answer.

402   You can see that God promised great blessing in this world when Christ comes back to rule as King for a thousand years, and we can be sure that God will fulfill His promises. Why then do some believers say there will be no Millennium? They say Christ rules as King in our hearts but He will never rule over the whole world.

These people teach that the Bible does not mean exactly what it says. The Bible says that:

1. The Lord will stand on the Mount of Olives, Zechariah 14.4.

2. Jerusalem will be the center of the world, Isaiah 2.2-4; Jeremiah 3.17.

3. The Lord will be there, Joel 3.17; Zechariah 8.2,3.

4. The Lord will rule there, Micah 4.7.

We must not change the plain meaning of a verse to make it fit in with our own ideas. We can be sure that the Lord Jesus will come again and rule as King over the earth for a thousand years.

Which of these statements is true?

1.   Christ rules in the hearts of believers, and God will never send Him into this world again.   FRAME 397

2.   Some believers change the meaning of many verses and teach that the Lord will not rule as King during the Millennium.   FRAME 403

3.   Many verses promise great blessing on earth but they really mean that believers are very happy in heaven.

FRAME 405

403   They do, but we should take the plain meaning of every verse and understand it so that it fits in with all the rest of the Bible. Go on to Frame 407.

404   This is true, but look again for another true statement.

405   Believers are happy in heaven but God said He would bless men here on the earth when Christ rules as King, and He will surely do it. Try again.

406   This is true, but did you find another true statement? If you understand both go on to Frame 408.

407   Everything on earth will be wonderful during the Millennium when Christ rules as King. The Millennium will last for 1,000 years, but then it will come to an end. Why will God bring the Millennium to an end when men are getting great blessing? Because He has something still better for them.

We have already read about the New Heaven and Earth, Frame 345. The new earth will be far better than this earth even during the Millennium. This earth has been under the curse of God because of sin. God's Son was crucified on this earth. Even after the Millennium men on the earth will rise up and rebel against God. For these reasons God will destroy the earth with fire and create a new one. Righteousness will rule in this world during the Millennium, but righteousness will live or *dwell* and be at home in the new earth, 2 Peter 3.13. This world is very old but it will be destroyed; the new world will last for ever.

Which of these statements is or are true?

1.   Christ will rule on this earth and nothing can be better than that.   FRAME 400

2.   God will destroy this world because of sin and create another where there will never be any sin.   FRAME 404

3.   In the Millennium everything will be wonderful but the new earth will be better still.   FRAME 406

408   We have learned many things about the Millennium in Lesson 8, but it is not necessary to add them to the Chart. You could look at Chart 7 again and read Frame 359. If you understand it well, you can go on to Frame 409 in Lesson 9.

9

GREAT LEADERS
OF THE FUTURE

409   We have seen that there will be a time of terrible trouble before the Lord Jesus comes back, Frame 192. Men will be deceived and will try to fight against God. Who will be the chief leaders in the world during the Great Tribulation before the Lord comes?

The Lord Jesus said that He had come with His Father's authority, but the people of Israel would not receive Him. He spoke about another person who will come on his own authority, John 5.43. The Lord said that the people of Israel will receive this man as their leader. Many other verses speak about a great leader who will come and will be accepted by the Jews. The Jews believe the Old Testament promises that Messiah would come and make them into a great nation. They reject the Lord Jesus Christ but will be willing to accept another messiah. God sent His Son to be the Saviour of Israel and He will not send another. This messiah will come on his own authority.

Which of these statements is true?

1.   God is very patient and He will send another messiah to Israel.   FRAME 411

2.   The Jews rejected Christ and will never accept anyone else who claims to be their Messiah.   FRAME 415

3.   In the Tribulation a leader will come to the Jews on his own authority and will be welcomed.   FRAME 418

410   Even in John's time there were many antichrists, and in
          the Tribulation many false christs will appear. Read
Matthew 24.24 and 1 John 2.18,22; 4.3 again, also Frame 412,
and look for the right answer.

411   No, this would dishonour His Son. God approved the Lord
          Jesus and will never give any man the same honour. Look
for a true statement.

412   The Antichrist

          The Lord also tells us many false christs or false messiahs
will appear at the time of the Tribulation. They will be able
to perform great miracles and will try to deceive God's people,
Matthew 24.24.

          Then the Holy Spirit tells us about the Antichrist, the great
enemy of Christ. Many antichrists will appear even before the last
days but at the end a great leader will appear, the Antichrist,
1 John 2.18,22; 4.3; 2 John 7. He will not only be the Enemy of
Christ, he will declare that he is the Messiah, sent to save the
world.

          *An educated man may come and tell you he is a Bible
teacher or a prophet from God. He may look nice and be very
kind. How can you know if he is real or not?* **By his teaching.**
*He may teach something new or different from the Bible. If
he does, this proves that he is not true. Of course, you have to
know the Bible so that you can tell when someone teaches
differently.*

          Read all the verses given and think about these statements.
Which one is correct?

  1. No antichrists have appeared in the past, but many will
     come in the Tribulation.   FRAME 410

  2. There will be many false christs and antichrists, but in
     the end a great leader will appear called the Antichrist.
                                                  FRAME 416

  3. Every enemy of Christ is an antichrist and there have
     always been many of them: the Pharisees, the

Sadducees, the heathen. It will be the same to the end.
FRAME 420

413 Far from it. There are many false prophets today and there
will be more after the Church has gone to heaven. The
Lord Jesus would not call them *false* prophets if God had sent
them. Read all of Frame 417 again and look for the right answer.

414 No, he will at first oppose the worship of all gods, then he
will tell men to worship him. Read the second part of
Frame 421 again.

415 The Lord Jesus taught that Israel **will** receive a man who
comes on his own authority. Read John 5.43 and Frame
409 again.

416 True; go to Frame 417.

417 The False Prophet
The Lord Jesus also said there will be many false prophets
in the time of the Tribulation, Matthew 24.11,24. They will teach
about religion and claim they have been sent by God, but it will be
a lie. John said that there were many false prophets in his time,
1 John 4.1.

Later the Holy Spirit spoke about **the** False Prophet. This
person will be so wicked that an evil spirit will come out of his
mouth, Revelation 16.13. This spirit will be able to do miracles
and will help bring all kings together to fight against God.

The False Prophet will be thrown alive into the lake of fire
together with another great leader called the Beast. The dragon or
the devil will also go there. They will be tormented for ever,
Revelation 19.20; 20.10.

Which of these statements is true?

1. Every prophet teaches about religion and we should
   believe that God sent him.   FRAME 413

2. The False Prophet will be a good man who will not
   understand God's ways very well.   FRAME 419

3.   There were many false prophets in John's time and there will be many more in the Tribulation. A great leader called the False Prophet will be punished for ever.

FRAME 423

418   This is true. Go to Frame 412.

419   No, the False Prophet will be a very evil man who will deceive people and turn them against God. He will be punished according to what he has done. Read the last two paragraphs of Frame 417 again.

420   Well, there are many enemies of Christ, but they will become very strong when the Church is taken up to heaven. So the Lord Jesus spoke about many false messiahs who will appear during the Tribulation. Read Mark 13.22 and study Frame 412 again.

421   The Man of Sin

We read about another great leader of the future in 2 Thessalonians 2. Read verses 3 and 4 and notice:

1. His name: He is called the Wicked One or the Man of Sin, because he will not obey God's law, vs.3,8. Of course there have always been many sinners and they will become worse and worse, 2 Timothy 3.13; but this man will be so evil that the Holy Spirit calls him **the** Wicked One.

2. He will first oppose everything which gives honour to the true God or even to any false god. Then he will put himself above all else, sit down in God's temple and claim that he himself should be worshipped, 2 Thessalonians 2.4.

God's law says plainly that we should never worship any man or spirit or image but only God the Creator of all. This future world leader is himself most wicked, and also makes other men commit terrible sin by worshipping him.

Which of these statements is or are true?

1.   The Man of Sin will tell people to worship their own gods, but not the God of heaven.   FRAME 414

2. The Wicked One will sit in the temple of Jehovah at Jerusalem as if he were God.   FRAME 424

3. The Man of Sin or the Wicked One will tell men not to worship God and will make them worship him.
FRAME 427

422   A miracle is something which no man can do in his own power. Satan has more power than men, but less than God. We should not follow people just because they can do some wonderful thing. They might have the power of Satan and lead us away from God. Read Frame 425 and the verses given there, then find the right answer.

423   You are right. Go to Frame 421.

424   This is true, but there is another statement after Frame 421 which is true. Be sure you understand both of them.

425   How could any man sit in the temple of God and tell people to worship him? The Wicked One will come and do this with the power of Satan. Satan has more power than any man but God has more power still. The Wicked One will be able to do great miracles and people will believe him and worship him. Read 2 Thessalonians 2.9-12.

The Wicked One will deceive millions of people but they are not innocent either. They did not love the truth and had decided before this that they did not want to be saved. So God will allow them to believe these lies. They refused to believe the truth, they loved their sins, they must be condemned.

You see how important it is for us to give people the truth and teach them to love it. Those who do not love the truth will later believe a terrible lie and follow the Man of Sin.

Think and choose:

1. Only God and His Son and His people can do real miracles.   FRAME 422

2.   Many people will want to be saved but will not have the opportunity to believe.   FRAME 426

3.   The Man of Sin will get power from Satan to do great miracles. He will be able to deceive many people and they will be condemned.   FRAME 428

426   No, God will save all who really want to be saved, unless they wait too long. God knows those who have refused Him and He will allow Satan to deceive them. Read Frame 425 again and get the right answer.

427   This is true. Did you find **two** true statements after Frame 421? If so, you may go to Frame 425.

428   This is true; go to Frame 429.

429   Of course God will also judge the Man of Sin who will deceive so many people. God knew long ago that this man would have to go to hell, 2 Thessalonians 2.3. The Lord Jesus will come with power and glory and destroy the Wicked One with His breath, v.8. So the Man of Sin will continue his wicked work only until the Lord comes.

When will the Man of Sin appear and start his evil work? The Man of Sin will appear at the time of the final rebellion against God. This is called the **Apostasy**, because millions of men will turn against God and against Christ. We will learn more about this in Frame 555.

Think and choose:

1.   The great Apostasy has already started and the Man of Sin will not be destroyed until Christ comes for His people.   FRAME 430

2.   God knew that the Man of Sin would have to go to hell; it would have been better if He had killed him before he became so wicked.   FRAME 432

3.   The Man of Sin will appear at the time of the great Apostasy and will continue only until the Lord comes in power and glory.   FRAME 436

430   Men have started already to turn from God, but the great Apostasy will take place after the Church has gone. Then the Man of Sin will rise up and continue until the Lord comes and destroys him. Read Frame 429 and try again.

431   There is already a great deal of wickedness in the world, sometimes we cannot understand how men can be so wicked. Still there is a power today that holds back wickedness and keeps it from spreading. Read 2 Thessalonians 2.6,7. This power is the power of the Holy Spirit, who will not always be on earth and try to help men, Genesis 6.3. The Holy Spirit came in a special way when the Church was formed on the day of Pentecost, Frame 241. He will stay with the Church on earth until we are taken to heaven. After that the Holy Spirit will not be here to hold back wickedness in the same way that He does now.

Think and choose:

1.   God the Holy Spirit is everywhere at once and He will always be here in this world.   FRAME 433

2.   The Holy Spirit prevents evil from spreading but He will not be here on earth in the same way after the Church has gone to heaven.   FRAME 435

3.   Governments are the power which holds back evil.
FRAME 439

432   God knows what all men will do but He does not **force** them to do what is wrong. We cannot blame God for the evil things which men do. If God killed one man Satan would find someone else to do his work. Look again for the right answer.

433   You are partly right, but the Holy Spirit came in a *special* way on the day of Pentecost to form the Church. He will go with the Church when it goes to heaven at the time of the Rapture. Then the power of evil will become stronger on earth. Read Frame 431 again and think about the right answer.

434   **The First Beast**
In Revelation 13.1-7 we read about another great world leader of the future. He is called the **first beast** because there

is another one in this same chapter. What can we learn about the first beast?

1. He will come up out of the sea, v.1. The sea is a picture of the wicked Gentile nations, Isaiah 57.20. The first beast will be a Gentile.

2. He will have seven heads and ten horns and ten crowns. The fourth beast in Daniel 7.7 had ten horns, and the dragon will have seven heads and ten horns and seven crowns, Revelation 12.3. So the first beast will be like the fourth king, the king of Rome; he will also be like Satan.

3. He also will look like three wild animals which were pictures of the first three empires in Daniel 7.3-6; Frame 139. The first beast will be a great Gentile king who will rule the world like the old kings Daniel spoke about.

Which of these statements is or are true?

1.　The first beast will have more power than Satan because he will have ten crowns and Satan will have only seven.
FRAME 437

2.　The first beast will be a Gentile king who will rule over the world empire of Rome.　FRAME 440

3.　The first beast makes us think of Satan and the four world rulers of Daniel 7.　FRAME 444

435　True; go to Frame 434.

436　True, go to Frame 431.

437　No, the ten crowns show that these horns are pictures of ten kings and the first beast will control them all. Satan is the ruler of the whole world, John 12.31; 14.30; 16.11. Go back to Frame 434 and try again.

438　What will the first beast do? John saw a wicked name on the seven heads of the beast, Revelation 13.1. This means that the first beast will openly oppose God and say terrible things about Him, vs.5,6. He will hate God and fight against His people; for a while he will be able to defeat them, v.7.

The first beast looked like the fourth king who had ten horns, Daniel 7.7. One of these horns spoke great things against God, Daniel 7.8,25. This little horn also attacked God's people until God came to save them, Daniel 7.21,22. So the first beast of Revelation 13 will be like the little horn of Daniel 7.

Which is true?

1. God will destroy the first beast as soon as he touches His beloved people.　　　　　　　　　　　FRAME 441

2. John read the book of Daniel and copied some of the things Daniel saw in a dream.　　　　　　FRAME 443

3. The first beast will be like the little horn: he will say terrible things against God and he will attack His people.
    　　　　　　　　　　　　　　　　　　FRAME 448

439　　Some people think that the Holy Spirit meant *Government* in 2 Thessalonians 2.6, and good governments do keep back evil. But verse 7 speaks about the *One* who holds back evil; this means one person, not a government. There will still be government during the Tribulation but the Church will be gone and the Holy Spirit will not use His power to hold back evil. Read Frame 431 again and find the right answer.

440　　This is true, but it is not the only true statement. Go back to Frame 434 and look for another one.

441　　No, God will let His people suffer for a while and some will be killed, Matthew 24.9. Then the Son of God will come and save His people, Daniel 7.22. He will raise from death those who died for Him, Revelation 20.4. You can find a better answer.

442　　Where will the first beast get his authority to do these things? From Satan, the dragon, Revelation 13.2. We have seen that the first beast will look like the dragon, Frame 434, paragraph 2. Satan wanted to be like God, Isaiah 14.13,14, and here we read that people will worship him. Everybody in the world will worship the first beast, except those who believe in the Lord Jesus Christ, vs.3,4,8.

But God will not allow the first beast to do these things very long. The first beast will have authority for only three and a half years or 42 months, v.5.

Choose one or two true statements:

1. Satan will give authority to the first beast and most men will worship both the beast and Satan.   FRAME 445

2. God will let men worship two of His creatures for three and a half years.   FRAME 447

3. Even today some people worship Satan and others worship a man or a woman.   FRAME 450

443   Some people say this, those who do not believe in the Bible. The Holy Spirit did show John many new things and we know that the Bible is true. Read Frame 438 again.

444   This is true because he looked like the dragon and the four wild animals which Daniel saw in his dream. Did you find the other true statement after Frame 434? If you understand both of them go on to Frame 438.

445   This is true. If you understand this go on to Frame 446.

446   The Second Beast
We read in Revelation 13.11-18 about another great world leader of the future. The second beast will come up out of the earth, v.11. We saw that the first beast came up out of the sea, a picture of the Gentile nations, Frame 434, paragraph 1. In the Bible the land often means the land of Israel, so we can believe that the second beast will be a Jew.

The second beast will have two horns like a lamb. In the book of Revelation you can find the word "Lamb" 29 times. It always means the Lord Jesus Christ except in 13.11. This person will look like a lamb and people will think that he is Christ, but he will speak like the dragon and his words show what he really is in his heart. Read Matthew 7.15-20.

*Our words also show what is in our hearts, Luke 6.45.
We should be very careful what we say, because Christ will
judge every evil word, Matthew 12.36,37.*

Which is true?

1. You can always tell what a person is really like by
   listening to what he says.   FRAME 449

2. The second beast will have two horns like the ram in
   Daniel 8.3, so the second beast is a picture of the king
   of Media and Persia.   FRAME 452

3. The second beast will be a Jew and people will think he
   is their Messiah. But Christ spoke the words His Father
   gave Him, John 8.28, and the second beast will speak
   the language of Satan.   FRAME 455

447   God will allow this, but you must not think that God will
      be too weak to stop them. He will send His Son to judge
Satan and all men. Read Frame 442 again.

448   This is true, go to Frame 442.

449   You can test any prophet or teacher by what he says; you
      will know when he starts teaching something different
from the Bible. But at first a false prophet speaks very nice words
and will try to deceive you. Look at Frame 446 again and pick out
a true statement which gives in short form what the Frame
teaches.

450   This is true, but it is very wrong and wicked. God will
      judge these people also when Christ comes. Go back to
Frame 442 and find the true statement which gives in short form
the main teaching of the Frame.

451   The second beast will have the same authority as the first
      beast, Revelation 13.12; the first beast will get this
authority from Satan, v.2. People will worship the first beast,
vs.4,8, and the second beast will make them do so, v.12. The
second beast will perform miracles by the power of Satan an'

deceive many people, vs.13,14. In these two things, the second beast will be like the Man of Sin, 2 Thessalonians 2.9,10.

God commanded us not to make an image or worship an idol, Exodus 20.4,5, but the second beast will tell men to make an image of the first beast and will force them to worship it, vs.14,15. This image will be able to breathe and talk and to kill all who refuse to worship it.

Think and choose: which of these statements is or are true?

1. The second beast will use his great power to make people worship him.   FRAME 453

2. The second beast will in some ways be like the first beast; in other ways he will be like the Man of Sin.
                                                                FRAME 456

3. The first beast will give his authority to the second beast and the second beast will deceive men and make them worship the image of the first beast.   FRAME 459

452   The ram was a picture of the king of Media and Persia, but this empire was destroyed by Greece long ago, Frame 157. The second beast is a picture of a great world ruler of the future. Look for a better answer.

453   No, most people will worship the first beast, v.8. The second beast will use his authority to make people worship the first beast and the image of the first beast, vs.12,15. Read Frame 451 again.

454   The Mark of the Beast
Then the second beast will do something else so that people will give honour to the first beast. He will make people receive a mark on the right hand or on the forehead. This mark will be on everybody, both rich people and poor, because no one will be able to buy food or anything else, nor sell anything, unless he has this mark. Only true believers will refuse to receive the mark. The mark will either be the name of the first beast or else his number. We do not know the name of the first beast, but his number will be 666.

In the Bible many numbers have a special meaning. For example, seven is the number of what is perfect. Six is the number of man, who always comes short of what God wants him to do. Before Christ comes, men will join together to fight against God, 19.19. The Man of Sin will sit in God's temple and people will worship him. The number 666 speaks of men opposed to God, as they are in Psalm 2.2,3. The second beast will make people receive this mark; he will bring men together and try to fight against God.

Which of these statements is or are true?

1. The number of man is 666 and the second beast will try to put it on everybody.   FRAME 457

2. Only rich people will be able to buy food without the mark of the beast.   FRAME 460

3. Before Christ comes, men will join together, worship a man, and try to get free from God's control.

FRAME 464

455   True. Now go to Frame 451 for more about the second beast.

456   This is true, but you can find another statement which explains Frame 451 in short form. This will show you which Frame to go to next.

457   This is true, but look for another true statement.

458   What will be the end of the two beasts of Revelation 13?
We read about the dragon, the beast, and the False Prophet in Revelation 16.13 and 20.10. In 19.20 we see that the False Prophet will perform miracles and deceive the people who will have the mark of the beast and worship his image. This is just what we read about the second beast in Revelation 13, so we see that the second beast is also called the False Prophet. He will be thrown alive into the lake of fire with the first beast, Frame 417.

We have also seen that the second beast will look like a lamb and people will accept him as the Messiah. But he will speak the words of Satan; from this we understand that he is really the Antichrist, Frame 412.

What do you think about these three statements? Which is or are true?

1. The two beasts of Revelation 13 will never die; they will be thrown alive into the Lake of Fire.   FRAME 461

2. The dragon, the beast and the False Prophet will be a trinity of evil just as God the Father, Son and Holy Spirit are the Trinity.   FRAME 463

3. The second beast is called the False Prophet and the Antichrist; he will be thrown alive into the Lake of Fire.
    FRAME 466

459   True. If this is clear go to Frame 454.

460   No, the second beast will force all people, rich and poor, to accept this mark. Only true believers will refuse and they will suffer for it. Look again for the right answer.

461   This is true, but look for another true statement which gives the teaching of Frame 458 in short form. It will tell you which Frame to go to next.

462   We have read in the Bible about several great leaders of the future, all enemies of God and Christ:

1. Someone who will come on his own authority and the Jews will receive him, Frame 409.

2. The Antichrist, who will claim to be the Saviour of the Jews, Frame 412.

3. The False Prophet who will help bring all men together to fight against God, Frame 417.

4. The Man of Sin who will sit in God's temple and people will worship him, Frames 421, 425, 429.

5. The first beast, who will attack God's people but will be worshipped by all other men, Frames 434, 438, 442.

6. The second beast who will perform miracles and tell people to worship the first beast, Frames 446, 451, 454.

We have seen that the Jews will receive the Antichrist who is also called the second beast or the False Prophet. He will be the great leader of the false Church and the religion of the future.

The first beast will be the great leader of the government of the world in the future. In many ways he will be like the Man of Sin, but the Lord Jesus will destroy the Man of Sin and throw the beast alive into the lake of fire, 2 Thessalonians 2.8; Revelation 19.20.

Which two statements are true?

1. In the future there will be two great leaders, one the political leader and the other the religious leader. These will be called the beast and the False Prophet or Antichrist.   FRAME 465

2. The two great leaders of the future will fight it out to find out which is the greater, and one will kill the other.   FRAME 467

3. The Jews will receive someone who will come on his own authority. This person is called in Scripture the Antichrist, the False Prophet and the second beast of Revelation 13.   FRAME 468

463 No, the word *Trinity* does not mean any three persons who work together with the same purpose. We can use the word *Trinity* for God the Father, God the Son, and God the Holy Spirit, because there is only one God. Satan and his two servants the beast and False Prophet will work together with the purpose of attacking God's people because they hate God. They are three persons; they are not **one** in the same way that God is one. People sometimes call Satan, the beast, and the False Prophet a trinity of evil, but they do not use the word trinity correctly. Look at Frame 458 and try again.

464 This is one of the two true statements after Frame 454. If you understand both of them, go to Frame 458.

465 This is true, now look also for another true statement.

466   True. If you have found and understood two true statements, go to Frame 462.

467   No, the False Prophet will help the beast and make people worship him. Neither of these men will be killed, but the Lord will throw them both alive into the lake of fire. Try again for the right answer.

468   This is also true. Did you find the other true statement? If so, go to Frame 469.

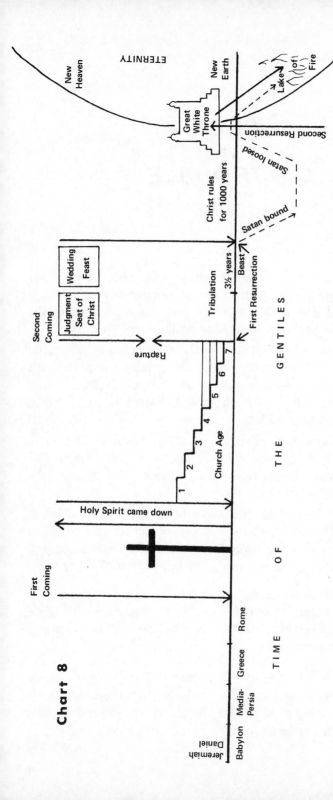

Chart 8

Jeremiah
Daniel

Babylon | Media-Persia | Greece | Rome

First Coming

Second Coming

Holy Spirit came down

Church Age

1 2 3 4 5 6 7

Rapture

| Judgment Seat of Christ | Wedding Feast |

Tribulation

First Resurrection

Beast

3½ years

Satan bound

Christ rules for 1000 years

Satan loosed

Second Resurrection

Great White Throne

Lake (of) Fire

TIME OF THE GENTILES

New Heaven

ETERNITY

New Earth

---

469   Now look at Chart 8. We have seen that the first beast will continue to rule over men for 3 1/2 years or 42 months, Frame 442. His rule will end when the Lord Jesus comes as King of kings. So we can show the Beast on the Chart. He will start to rule 3 1/2 years before Christ comes and throws him into the lake of fire.

If you understand the Chart go right on to Frame 470 in Lesson 10.

10

HALF A WEEK

OF TROUBLE

470 We will now look more closely at some verses in the Bible which speak about the time of terrible trouble. This is called the Great Tribulation and will take place just before the Lord Jesus comes back to rule as King on the earth.

Daniel wrote a little about the Great Tribulation. The little horn will come speaking proud words and making war with God's people for three and a half times or years, Daniel 7.20,21,25,26. A fierce king will rise in the last days and destroy many of God's holy people, Daniel 8.23,24.

The Lord Jesus told us still more about this time of trouble for the Jews. Read Matthew 24.9-22 and read again Frame 192 about the Great Tribulation; also Frame 196 about the Abomination of Desolation.

This will be the worst time of trouble in the history of Israel, Daniel 12.1. The Lord Jesus said it would be the greatest tribulation and the worst trouble in the history of the world, Matthew 24.21. We can call it **the** Great Tribulation.

The Lord Jesus called us His friends because He tells us in Scripture what He is going to do. We ought to warn our friends and relatives about the terrible time of tribulation which is coming soon.

Think and choose one or more true statements:

1. The Holy Spirit spoke through Daniel, and the Lord Jesus taught the same thing: there will be terrible trouble for Israel just before the Lord comes again.

FRAME 472

2. The worst trouble will begin when the Abomination of Desolation is set up in the holy temple of God, and the Jews in Jerusalem should then run away to the hills.

FRAME 474

3. Israel will have a lot of trouble, but other nations have had still more. FRAME 477

471 This is true, but look again for another true statement.

472 This is true, but there is another true statement.

473 You are right. Now look for another true statement.

474 This is true. If you had read Frame 196 again you would remember what it says. There are two true statements after Frame 470. If you got them both go on to Frame 475.

475 The Book of Revelation tells us many things about the Great Tribulation. We have already looked at chapters 2 and 3 which give us in short form the history of the Church during the entire Church Age. See Lesson 6. We have also studied chapters 19-21, and learned many things about the coming of the Lord and the future, Lesson 7. Revelation 4-18 tell us about what will take place **after** the Church Age and **before** the Lord comes in power and glory. What can we learn about the Great Tribulation in these chapters?

First notice that chapters 4 and 5 give us a picture of heaven. Then in chapter 6.1-17 and 8.1 we read what will happen when seven seals are broken. In 8.6 to 9.21 and 11.15-19 seven angels blow seven trumpets and terrible things happen. But in chapter 16 we read about seven angels who will pour out seven bowls of God's anger on the earth. This will be the worst of all.

Write in your own words what we can find in the Book of Revelation. What do we read in:

Chapters 2 and 3? _____

Chapters 4 and 5? _____

Chapter 6?   _____

Chapters 8 and 9?   _____

Chapter 13?   _____

Chapter 16?   _____

Chapters 19–21?   _____

Have you written down what each part contains? When you have, turn to Frame 490 and see if you got the right answers.

476   The Seven Seals

John saw a book in heaven which was sealed like an envelope with seven seals. Only the Lord Jesus could open the seals, Revelation 5.1-10.

The Lord opened the first seal and a man appeared on a white horse; he had the authority to conquer and rule over many nations, Revelation 6.1,2.

The Lord opened three more seals and other men came riding on horses. The second brought war on the earth, vs.3,4. The third brought famine and there was not enough food for men, vs.5,6. The fourth man had authority to kill one man out of four of all men on earth, vs.7,8.

Some believers were killed and when the Lord broke the fifth seal they asked how much longer they would have to wait before God would punish their enemies, vs.9-11.

Then the Lord broke the sixth seal and the kings and rulers were afraid because they knew the day of the Lord's anger was coming very soon.

Think about these things:

1.   There have always been wars and famines on earth but while the Lord breaks these six seals, things will get worse and worse.   FRAME 471

2.   Four men will come on four horses. They will bring trouble to men on earth.   FRAME 478

3.   The Lord can open the book of the living and men will be blessed when He does so.   FRAME 480

477   The Great Tribulation will be the worst time of trouble in the history of the world and no nation has ever had as much. God will pour out His anger on Israel and all nations. Read the last part of Frame 470 again and look for two true statements.

478   This is true. Did you find another true statement? If so, go on to Frame 479.

479   The First Four Trumpets

The Lord opened the seventh seal and this started the next series, the seven trumpets, 8.1-6. The trumpets brought still greater trouble on earth.

The time of the seven seals will be like the first part of Matthew 24, which is called the beginning of Pain, Frame 186. The trumpets and bowls will be like the second part of Matthew 24, called the Great Tribulation, Frame 192.

The first four angels will blow their trumpets one after another, 8.7-12. Read these verses and answer the questions.

1. What will happen to the trees? _____

2. What will happen to the fish? _____

3. What will happen to the rivers? _____

4. What will happen to day and night? _____

Look up your answers in the Bible and write them in your book; then turn to Frame 496 to see if you got everything right.

480   The book with seven seals is not the same as the book of the living, Revelation 21.27. The Lord opened the seals and great trouble started to come to men. Read Frame 476 again very carefully.

481   No, one out of three of all men will be killed, but even then the rest will not repent of their sins. We should not tell God what to do, as if we were wiser than He. Read Frame 485 again and find the true statements.

482   This is true. After the sixth trumpet one out of three of all
men will die, but there are worse things than death, 9.6,
and men will go through terrible torture when the bowls of God's
wrath are poured out. Look for another true statement.

483   This is also true. If you understand both true statements,
go on to Frame 488.

484   The Fifth Trumpet
After the fourth angel blows his trumpet, an eagle says
that there will be horrible things on earth when the other three
angels blow their trumpets, 8.13.

The fifth angel will blow his trumpet and millions of locusts
will come to torture men for five months. These locusts will come
from the *abyss*, 9.1-3, and the name of their king is Destroyer,
v.11. Read Luke 8.31 and think of one or two words to finish this
statement:

The locusts in Revelation 8 are a picture of . . . .

Write your answer in your book and then turn to Frame 491
to see if you understand this question.

485   The Last Two Trumpets
The sixth angel will blow his trumpet and four other
angels will be released, Revelation 9.13-19. These angels are
prepared for this very time and their work will be to kill one
person out of three of all people in the world.

Surely you would think that the other people would turn
from their sins when they see that millions have died. Not so,
vs.20,21. When the Lord breaks the sixth seal, kings and rulers will
be afraid, but when the sixth angel blows his trumpet men will
refuse to repent.

After this John saw several visions; then the seventh angel
blew his trumpet, 11.15-19. This will be just before the Lord
comes and starts to rule over the whole world. Still people on
earth will not be ready to accept Him, and God will pour out still
more judgment upon men.

Think and choose:

1.   One person out of three of all people will be killed, but even then men will not repent nor be willing to receive Christ as King.   FRAME 473

2.   Why does God let wicked men live? God should punish a few sinners and then the rest would turn to Him.   FRAME 481

3.   Men in heaven will be very happy when Christ is ready to come and rule, but men on earth will oppose Him.   FRAME 483

4.   A God of love will never kill millions of people at one time.   FRAME 486

486   Yes, He will. God will punish men for their sins during the Great Tribulation. Read Frame 485 again and look for the right answer.

487   This is true, but God will judge men for listening to evil spirits. If you understand two true statements, turn to Frame 493.

488   **Five Bowls of Wrath**

John saw several other visions in Revelation 12-14, and we have studied the two beasts who are described in chapter 13. In chapter 15 we could read about the seven angels with the seven last plagues. They will be given seven bowls filled with the wrath of God, and in chapter 16 they will pour out God's wrath on the earth.

1. Terrible sores will appear on those who have the mark of the beast.
2. All fish will die.
3. Rivers will turn into blood.
4. The sun will burn men with its heat.
5. Darkness will come over the whole earth.

Read 16.1-11 and fill in the right answer:

1. After the .... bowl, men on earth will curse God.

2. After the .... bowl, men will bite their tongues because of their pain.

3. After the .... bowl praise is given to God.

Write your answers in your book, then turn to Frame 492 to see if you understand this Frame.

489   The Sixth and Seventh Bowls

The sixth angel will pour out his bowl, Revelation 16.12-14. The great river Euphrates will dry up so the kings of Asia can cross. Wicked spirits will gather men together to fight against God. We have seen what will happen to these men when Christ comes, Frame 313.

Finally the last angel will pour out his bowl into the air, 16.17-21. Then there will be a terrible earthquake, the worst since Adam was created. Great hail stones will fall from the sky on men and they will curse God again, as they will do after the fourth bowl and the fifth bowl, and a loud voice will call out of heaven, *IT IS DONE.*

What do you think? Which of these statements are true?

1.   The seven trumpets will bring more trouble on men than the seven seals, but the seven bowls will be worse still.
FRAME 482

2.   Evil spirits will persuade men to fight against God.
FRAME 487

3.   The seventh angel will pour out the seventh bowl of God's wrath, and then Christ will come.   FRAME 494

490   Chapters 2 and 3   History of the Church Age in short form.

Chapters 4 and 5   A picture of heaven

Chapter 6   Six seals will be broken

Chapters 8 and 9   The seventh seal will be broken and six angels will blow their trumpets.

Chapter 13   The beast and the Anti-Christ

Chapter 16   Seven angels pour out seven bowls of God's anger.

Chapters 19-21   The Coming of the Lord and the
                    future.

Your answer is correct if you wrote in your book words which mean about the same as the answer given here. When you understand this Frame go to Frame 476 and we will look more closely at these chapters in Revelation.

491   The evil spirits or demons asked the Lord not to send them at once into the abyss, Luke 8.31. So these locusts are a picture of demons who will come to torture men for five months during the Great Tribulation. Now turn to Frame 485.

492   After the fourth and fifth bowls men on earth will curse God. After the fifth bowl men will bite their tongues because of pain. After the third bowl praise will be given to God. If you understand these answers go to Frame 489.

493   How long will the Great Tribulation last?

We have seen that the time of trouble will be in two parts, the second far worse than the first. (If you are not sure about this, read Frame 479, first paragraph.)

1. The beginning of Pain, or the seven seals.

2. The Great Tribulation, or the seven trumpets and seven bowls.

Sometimes the words *Great Tribulation* are used for the whole time of trouble, but the second part will be far worse than the first.

We have also seen that the beast will rule over the world for 42 months or three and a half years, Revelation 13.5, Frame 442. The beast will speak against God, accept worship from men, and kill God's people. God will pour out His judgment on men at that time because of their sins.

How long will the Great Tribulation last? _____

Why do you think so? _____

Write in your answers, then turn to Frame 501.

494   Not at once. God will judge Babylon, the great prostitute, chapters 17 and 18, and Christ will come when all men are gathered together to fight against God, 19.19. Look again for your answer.

495   You are right, and we should not say that these times are exact. However, God will protect the woman Israel for 1,260 days or for three and a half times or years, Revelation 12.6,14, so these two time periods are the same. The important thing is that these events will all happen during the same period. Read Frame 497 again and look for another answer.

496   One third of the trees will be burned up. One third of the fish will die. One third of the rivers will turn into bitter poison. There will be no light for one third of day and night. Do you understand these answers? If so, go to Frame 484.

497   There are other verses in Revelation 11 and 12 which speak about a period of 42 months:

1. The Gentiles will control Jerusalem for 42 months, 11.2.

2. God's two witnesses will give His message to people for 1,260 days, 11.3. Each month has 30 days, so 42 months will be the same as 1,260 days.

3. God will take care of a woman in the desert for 1,260 days, 12.6 This is the same as three and a half times or years, 12.14. (This woman is a picture of Israel and Satan will attack her because Christ was born in Israel.)

Think and choose:

1.   Some months have 31 days and one has only 28 or 29, so three and a half years are really 1,278 days.
FRAME 495

2.   For three and a half years the Gentile beast will control Jerusalem and many people of Israel will have to flee.
FRAME 498

3.   God will take care of Israel and He will look after His two witnesses for 42 months or 1,260 days. FRAME 502

498   This is true. Look for another true statement.

499   Christ died and can make believers righteous before God,
but there is a great deal of evil in the world today. Christ
will bring in everlasting righteousness for Israel and for the world
when He comes again. Many other prophecies have not yet been
fulfilled so we cannot say that the 70 weeks have been completed.
Read the second part of Frame 500 and look again for a true
statement.

500   The Seventy Weeks

We must now turn to a very important prophecy which
God gave to Daniel. Read Daniel 9.24-27; read these verses again
about five times. The first part of this chapter shows that Daniel
really prayed that God would bless Israel and the Lord sent the
angel Gabriel to show him these things.

First Daniel learned that God had marked out 70 *weeks* or 70
times seven years, a total of 490 years, v.24. (In the Bible a *week*
may mean seven days or seven years.) By the end of 490 years
Christ must die to make reconciliation and bring in everlasting
righteousness. We know that our Lord has died for our sins,
Romans 5.10,11, and He will bring in everlasting righteousness
when He comes to rule over the world, Isaiah 32.1; Jeremiah
23.5,6.

Which of these statements is true?

1.   Christ brought in everlasting righteousness when He died
for our sins, so the 70 weeks were completed at His first
coming.   FRAME 499

2.   God told Daniel about a 490 year period for Israel. Part
of this prophecy has been fulfilled and part of it is still
future.   FRAME 503

501   The beast will rule for three and a half years and God will
send terrible trouble on men for their sins. It seems that
the Great Tribulation will last about the same length of time. We
will now look at other verses in Daniel and Revelation which speak
about the length of the Tribulation period. Turn to Frame 497.

502   This is true, one of the two true statements. If you understand them both go to Frame 500.

503   This is correct. Go on to Frame 504.

504   The Lord also told Daniel that this period of 490 years would start at the time when the king gave permission to build Jerusalem again, v.25; Nehemiah 2.1-8. Read these verses carefully and write down the name of this king. _____

The 70 weeks are divided into three periods: seven weeks, 62 weeks, and one week. Daniel 9.25 really means that there would be 69 weeks until the time of Christ, the Anointed One. After the 62 weeks Christ would be removed, v.26; He died on the cross.

Which of these statements is true or are they all wrong?

1.   Christ came 49 years after Jerusalem was built again.

                                          FRAME 505

2.   Daniel's 70 weeks were fulfilled soon after Christ died.

                                          FRAME 507

3.   About 483 years passed from the time of King Artaxerxes to the time Christ died.   FRAME 509

505   Some Bibles say seven weeks will pass until the anointed Prince comes but the old Hebrew Bible says from the word to build Jerusalem to the time of Messiah, there will be seven weeks and 62 weeks. This is what really happened; King Artaxerxes began to rule about 464 years before Christ was born. Look again at Frame 504 and find the true statement.

506   Next Daniel said a ruler would come against Jerusalem and against the temple, Daniel 9.26. We can read old books of history and see that Jerusalem was destroyed about 70 years after Christ was born. But verse 27 says that this coming ruler will make an agreement with the people of Israel for one week or seven years. After three and a half years the week will be half over and he will break his agreement and stop the Jews from offering sacrifices to God. Then there will be abominations and desolation.

The Lord Jesus told the Jews that they will see the

Abomination of Desolation or the Awful Horror, Matthew 24.15; Frame 196. This will be just before the world ruler starts to attack Israel. He will be allowed to kill many of God's people before Christ comes. So there will be three and a half years from the Abomination of Desolation until the Lord returns. We see that Daniel 9.26,27 will be fulfilled in the future.

Think and choose:

1.   The coming prince will make an agreement with the Jews and break it after about three and a half years.
                                                    FRAME 508

2.   The coming prince will set up an abomination in the temple and will stop the Jews from offering sacrifices to God.   FRAME 510

3.   The coming prince will be able to fight against God's people for three and a half years, then the Lord will come and destroy him.   FRAME 512

507   No prince made an agreement with the Jews soon after Christ died and then broke it after three and a half years. We shall see that this is still in the future. Find a true statement after Frame 504.

508   True, but look for another one.

509   This is true; go to Frame 506.

510   This is true, but can you find another one?

511   Let us now put down in order a few of the important things which we have learned about the Tribulation.

   1. One week of seven years is still future, Frame 506.

   2. It cannot start until the Church has gone to heaven, Frame 431.

   3. The Man of Sin or the beast will make an agreement with the Jews, Frame 506.

   4. There will be trouble in the world, the beginning of Pain, Frames 186, 479.

5. Half way through the seven years the beast will break his promise, Frame 506.

6. The beast will set up an idol called the Abomination of Desolation in the temple of God and all Jews should run away as quickly as possible, Frame 196.

7. The False Prophet will tell people to worship the beast and the beast will sit in the temple of God, Frames 451, 421.

8. God will pour out terrible judgment because of men's sins, Frames 479, 484, 485, 488, 489.

9. The beast and the False Prophet will persecute the people of God and kill many of them, Frames 196, 204, 438.

10. The beast and the False Prophet will gather men and kings together to fight against God, Frames 313, 489.

11. The Lord will destroy these wicked men in a minute and throw the beast and the False Prophet into the lake of fire, Frame 318.

Now you can answer these three questions:

1. Why do we call the Great Tribulation *Half a Week of Trouble?*

_____

_____ FRAME 513

2. Who will suffer during the Great Tribulation, Christians, Jews,

or Gentiles? _____ FRAME 515

3. Why do they have to suffer? _____

_____

_____ FRAME 517

512   This is true and so are the other statements after Frame 506. If you understand these three statements go to Frame 511.

513   Seven years are called one week and the last half will be a
time of terrible trouble. It will really be three and a half
years long. Go back to Frame 511 and answer question 2.

514   Some people think that the Church too will go through the
Tribulation or part of the Tribulation. Others say that part
of the Church will suffer here on earth during the Tribulation
while the rest is in heaven. Let us think about these questions.

Will the Church go through the Tribulation? Some believers
say that the Church is very worldly and cold today, so God will
punish Christians for their sins during the Tribulation and make
the Church pure and ready for heaven.

True, the Church today is like the Laodicean Church, Frame
299, and there are many people in the churches who say that they
are Christians but do not really believe in the Lord. Real Christians
were made ready to go to heaven when they first trusted in Christ,
John 5.24, and God will punish us at once if we go on in sin,
Hebrews 12.5-11.

Why does God promise to keep us from the Tribulation?
Are we better than others, or do we love God more than
they? No, it is only the grace of God. We cannot boast or
become proud because God has chosen us in Christ. We
should thank Him for it and try to serve Him better.

Think and choose:

1.   We must go through the fire of tribulation before we are
      pure enough to stand before God.   FRAME 516

2.   Christ is preparing His Church like a Bride, Ephesians
      5.26,27. He does this by loving care and through the
      Word of God, not by tribulation and punishment.
                                                FRAME 519

3.   God planned the Tribulation period to punish Jews and
      Gentiles, not the Church.   FRAME 521

515   Jews and Gentiles. The Gentile beast will persecute the
Jews and God will pour out His wrath on all nations.

Revelation 6.8; 9.18. All true Christians will be in heaven. Go back to Frame 511 and answer question 3.

516   No, Christ died for our sins and we do not have to pay anything. God has already made us fit to share in the kingdom of light, Colossians 1.12. The Tribulation is not planned to punish or to purify the Church. Look again for the right answer.

517   Why do Jews and Gentiles have to suffer?

1. Jews and Gentiles will suffer because God will punish them for rejecting His Son the Lord Jesus Christ.

2. God will punish men because they worship the beast and the image of the beast, Revelation 14.9,10.

3. God will punish men for killing His people, Revelation 6.9-11.

4. God has tried and tested men under many conditions and they have always failed. But someone may say that God should punish sinners at once, then other men would fear Him and obey Him. So in the Great Tribulation God will pour out His wrath on men but still they will hate Him and fight against Him, Revelation 16.10,11,14.

If you got one or more of these answers, you did well. Think about the others, then go to Frame 514.

518   Other believers teach that only part of the Church will have to go through the Tribulation. They always mean others, who they think are less spiritual and more worldly than themselves. They use verses from the Bible which they say will prove this teaching.

For example, the Lord Jesus told His disciples to pray for strength to help them go through the Tribulation, Luke 21.36; but He was speaking to Jews, not Christians.

In Revelation 3.10 the Lord promised to keep some believers from the time of trouble: those who keep His order to be patient. From this verse you might think that all others will have to go through the Tribulation. But the Lord gave promises in other letters which are for **all** believers, not just for those in one church; for example, 2.7,11; 3.5. The promise in 3.10 is also for **all** believers.

Think and choose:

1. We should pray for strength to go through the Great Tribulation, Luke 21.36. FRAME 520

2. Only a few of the Christians of Ephesus will eat the fruit of the tree of life, Revelation 2.7. FRAME 522

3. Most believers will be hurt by the second death, but not those who win the victory in this life, Revelation 2.11. FRAME 526

4. Christ will remove from the book of life the names of all who do not win the victory, Revelation 3.5. FRAME 528

5. Some verses seem to teach that part of the Church will have to go through the Tribulation but we can understand what they really mean if we study them closely. FRAME 524

519 This is true. Is there another true statement?

520 No, the Lord gave this command to Jewish disciples, not to His Church. Read Frame 518, paragraph 2.

521 This is true. But remember, God will punish us here and now if we continue to sin against Him. God's grace does not mean that we can do as we please. He wants us to be pure and holy. If you found two true statements go to Frame 518.

522 We know that the tree of life is for all true believers, Revelation 22.2,14,19. In the same way the Lord will keep His whole Church from the time of trouble. Read Frame 518 again, the third paragraph.

523 There are other verses which prove that the Church will not go through the Tribulation:

1. We shall all be changed when the Lord comes, 1 Corinthians 15.51. This means all Christians, not just those who are spiritual.

2. Some people say that unspiritual believers have to go through the Great Tribulation; if so, unspiritual believers who have died should also be punished or made pure by tribulation. But the Bible says that those who died believing in Christ will rise from death when He comes, 1 Thessalonians 4.16.

3. Believers will get rewards or crowns for serving the Lord, Frames 84, 230. But the Rapture is not a reward for serving the Lord. It is an act of God answering the prayer of the Lord Jesus when He asked the Father that we might be with Him where He is, John 17.24.

Think and choose the statements which are true:

1. The Lord and the Church could be quite happy at the Wedding Feast, even if many members of Christ's Body were still in the world suffering terrible things during the Great Tribulation.   FRAME 525

2. Some believers think that part of the Church will have to go through the Tribulation, but there are many verses which show that this is not true.   FRAME 527

3. Spiritual Christians will be changed when the Lord comes for His Church.   FRAME 529

4. After they die all believers have to go to the Fire to make them pure and ready for heaven. So those who are still alive will have to go through the Tribulation.   FRAME 530

5. The Rapture is a reward for those believers who truly love the Lord and serve Him.   FRAME 531

6. Many members of the churches are not really saved and they will not go to heaven when the Lord comes. They will go through the Tribulation but will not turn to God or believe on the Lord Jesus.   FRAME 532

524   Good, go to Frame 523.

525   No, the Lord Jesus will not be fully happy until His Bride, all His Church, is with Him forever. Some believers will suffer during the Tribulation, but they will not be members of His Body, the Church. They will get a special reward when Christ comes with power and glory. Look for a true statement.

526   No, the second death is the lake of fire, Revelation 20.14, and only the wicked will be put into it. In Revelation 2.11 the Lord gives this promise to those who win the victory. Try again for a true statement.

527   This is correct. Look for another true statement.

528   No, He has given eternal life to all who believe in Him. Look again for a true statement.

529   All Christians will be changed and caught up to meet the Lord in the air, 1 Corinthians 15.51; 1 Thessalonians 4.17. Go back and find the true statements.

530   The Roman Catholic priests teach that all baptized members have to go to a fire called *purgatory* when they die. They say that our good works will make up for our sins, but no one has done enough good works. So everyone will suffer in purgatory until he is clean and pure enough for heaven.... Of course this is not in the Bible at all. We are saved because the work of Christ is enough to make all of us ready for heaven.

The second part of this statement is also false: the precious blood of Christ makes us ready for heaven, not our own suffering. Think about the other statements after Frame 523 and find those that are true.

531   No, the Lord will give rewards at the Judgment Seat of Christ to those who have served Him well, but the Rapture is the Lord's way of taking all believers to heaven. Look again for the true statements.

532   This is true. Did you find the other true statement? If you understand these questions go to Frame 533.

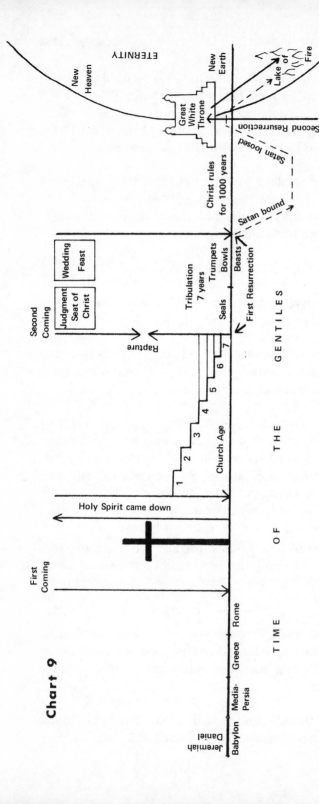

533 Look at Chart 9. We can now add several words to the Chart. Notice that the seven seals will be opened during the first part of the Tribulation. Later the seven angels will blow their trumpets and seven other angels pour out seven bowls of God's wrath on man. Two beasts will attack God's people.

Do you understand this Chart? Test yourself by answering the questions on Chart 9, page 179.

QUESTIONS ON CHART 9

Write your answers on a piece of paper.

1. Name the first Gentile kingdom which Daniel prophesied about. Which is the last one?

2. When did the time of the Gentiles start?   When will it end?

3. When did the Church Age start and when will it end?

4. How many periods of church history will continue until the end of the age?

5. What do we call the first part of Christ's second coming?

6. What will happen first in heaven after we get there?

7. What will happen on earth when the Church is gone?

8. Which will come first, bowls, seals, or trumpets? How many are there of each of these?

9. What will happen in heaven after the Lord gives crowns and rewards to those who have served Him well?

10. What will happen to the two beasts when the Lord comes? What about Satan?

11. How long will the Lord Jesus rule as King on this earth?

12. Where will God finally put Satan?

13. Where do people go after they are judged at the Great White Throne?

14. How long will the new Heaven and Earth last?

Check your answers on page 179.

RIGHT NOW

534 When you see a black cloud in the sky you know it is going to rain. In the evening people see that the sky is red and say the weather will be good. If the sky is red in the morning we can expect that it will rain. You can tell from the wind if it is going to get hotter or colder.... Read Matthew 16.2,3; Luke 12.54,56.

No man can tell what will happen in the future, except a prophet of God. But things happening today may help us to get ready for what will happen next. We do not know when the Lord will come for His Church, but we know from Scripture what will take place right after that, during the Tribulation. The world is being prepared now for what will happen soon.

In Lessons 11 and 12 we will read a few verses which speak about the "last time" or the "last days", and we will ask if any of these things are happening today. If they are, we may think that the Lord will soon come for us.

Think and choose:

1. We know from Scripture what will happen in the Tribulation, but the Rapture will take place first so we should not look at world events today.   FRAME 536

2. We can tell in advance when the weather is going to change and the Lord said we should be able to interpret what the Bible says.   FRAME 538

3. Satan can cause things to happen today and he will deceive those who are looking for events which show that Christ will soon come.   FRAME 541

535   Yes, these things show that we are in the last days. Go to Frame 543.

536   Conditions in the world can change very rapidly but still we can understand which way things are going. The Tribulation may start right after the Rapture. We may see today the beginning of what will happen soon after the Church is taken. Read Frame 534 again and look for a true statement.

537   No, far from it. What kind of spirits did you read about in 1 Timothy 4.1? Try again for the correct answer.

538   True. We can see things happening today which make us believe that the Lord will come soon. We should not look for these signs, but for the Lord Himself. He promised a crown to those who love Him and wait for Him to appear, 2 Timothy 4.8. Now go on to Frame 539.

539   The Holy Spirit in the New Testament often uses these words: the "last day" or the "last days" or the "last times."

1. We can know the end is near when many antichrists appear. They are special enemies of Christ, 1 John 2.18.

2. In the last days men will make fun of believers and laugh at our Lord's promise to return, 2 Peter 3.3,4; Jude 18.

3. Our salvation will be revealed at the end of time, 1 Peter 1.5. This will take place when our Saviour comes.

4. The Lord taught that He will raise believers from death on the last day, John 6.39,40,44,54; 11.24.

Today many people laugh when we tell them the Lord is coming back. Others follow false leaders or messiahs, who say they can save the world from trouble.

Do these things mean we are in the last days? What is your answer?

> 1. Yes   .... FRAME 535
>
> 2. No   .... FRAME 542
>
> 3. I don't know   .... FRAME 544

540   No, they try to deceive people. Why does Satan try to look like an angel, 2 Corinthians 11.13,14? Try again.

541   Satan can cause things to happen but he would not give men any reason to hope that Christ will soon come back again. He deceives men into thinking that they have plenty of time so they will not want to come to Christ until it is too late. Look for the true statement.

542   Why not? The Holy Spirit said these things would take place in the last days. We see them today, so we must understand that these are the last days. Read Frame 539 again and you will find the true statement.

543   Another proof of the last times is in 1 Timothy 4.1: men will leave the faith and reject the Bible because they obey lying spirits and demons.

Who are these spirits? There are many spirits in the world who do not love or obey God. They follow Satan and are the enemies of Christ and the people of God. Of course they do not tell people they are the enemies of Christ. Even Satan likes to look like an angel of light, 2 Corinthians 11.13,14. How can we know a spirit is evil? By what the spirit teaches. Demons and evil spirits do not teach the truth as the Bible teaches. You should not believe any man who teaches differently from the Bible.

Which of these statements is true?

1.   All spirits love God and tell us about Him. FRAME 537

2.   People who obey demons will always tell you who taught them.   FRAME 540

3.   Spirits are wiser than men and we cannot tell which ones are evil.   FRAME 545

4.   None of the first three statements is true.   FRAME 547

5.   All of the first three statements are true.   FRAME 549

544   No one can be certain when the Lord will come, but it seems that the day must be near. Read Frame 542 and think about Frame 539 again.

545   We can tell evil spirits and false teachers by their teaching. Is it what the Bible teaches? If not, do not believe them or follow them. Try again for a true statement.

546   Some people talk a lot in words which they cannot understand. Afterwards they say it made them feel wonderful and that it must have been the Holy Spirit who gave them this power. But this is not true. Evil spirits certainly have this power and they deceive people and make them think God is talking to them. Try again.

547   Correct. Go to Frame 548.

548   Spirits speak through mediums, witches or witch doctors. Sometimes a medium will say you can get a message from someone who has died. Do not listen to them. The Bible says we should not listen to witches or ask them questions, Deuteronomy 18.10-12. Sometimes an evil spirit comes on a person and makes him say many things he does not understand at all.

Satan will be thrown down to the earth in the middle of the Tribulation period, and all his wicked angels with him, Revelation 12.7-9. Even now he knows that his time is short, so he is sending many evil spirits to deceive men, if possible.

There are thousands of mediums and witches in North America and Great Britain today. Evil spirits are more active than ever and this fact tells us that we are in the last days of this age.

Think and choose:
1.   Only the Holy Spirit can make a person speak many words which he cannot understand.   FRAME 546
2.   After they die great men can tell us through mediums what to do.   FRAME 550
3.   Educated people would never believe in evil spirits or listen to witches.   FRAME 552

4.   All of the first three statements are true.   FRAME 554

5.   None of the above statements is true.   FRAME 556

549   Do you really think statements 1, 2 and 3 are all true? Look up the Frame numbers given after each statement and think more carefully about what the Bible says.

550   No, the medium may say that some great man is sending a message, but we should not believe it. Read Deuteronomy 18.10-12 again and look for a better answer.

551   The Conflict of the Ages

In the beginning God created all angels and spirits. Satan was at first an angel of God, but then he became proud and sinned against God, Isaiah 14.12-15; Ezekiel 28.11-16. God judged Satan at once and Satan has been God's enemy ever since.

1. He tempted Eve in the Garden of Eden and told her to sin, Genesis 3.

2. Cain belonged to Satan and he led him to murder his brother Abel, 1 John 3.12.

3. He accused Job to God and tries to accuse us also, Job 1.9-11; 2.4,5; Revelation 12.10.

4. He tried to tempt the Lord Jesus Christ, Matthew 4.1-11; Luke 4.1-13.

5. He will hate all who believe in God and will try to kill the people of Israel during the Great Tribulation, Revelation 12.13 (the woman is a picture of Israel). Satan will give his authority to the beast and the beast will kill many of God's people, Revelation 13.4,7.

6. At the end he will be thrown into the lake of fire and kept there forever, Revelation 20.10.

Think and choose:

1.   God created an evil spirit and he has been fighting against God ever since.   FRAME 553

2.   Satan is fighting against God and we still do not know who will win the final victory.   FRAME 557

3.   The conflict of the ages is the great struggle between God and Satan.   FRAME 559

4.   Satan hates God, but he tries to be kind to God's people so he can persuade them to follow him.   FRAME 561

552   Today many educated people ask witches and mediums for help and advice, but this is a sin. It shows we are in the last days. Look again for a true statement.

553   No, God created Satan and all the angels and they were all good at first. When Satan fell many angels followed him. The struggle began when Satan sinned. Read Frame 551, paragraph 1 again.

554   No, not at all; none of these is true. Surely you did not make three mistakes and think that all three were true! Read Frame 548 again and the Frame numbers given after the statements at the end.

555   Wicked spirits will deceive men and lead them away from God. Men will give up their faith in God and believe these lying spirits, 1 Timothy 4.1. Many people in the last days will be religious but will reject the Lord Jesus Christ, 2 Timothy 3.1,5. Satan will prepare men for the final rebellion. The man of sin will appear and lead the nations against God, 2 Thessalonians 2.3.

Today there are millions of true Christians in many churches around the world. They will all go to heaven when the Lord calls them at the time of the Rapture. The churches will be left behind and will soon turn away from the name of Christ. This is called the **Apostasy**. Now many people say they are Christians; after the Rapture they will join a new religion which will not accept Christ at all.

You can see how important it is that we should have nothing to do with spirits. These spirits may seem very interesting and helpful but they are controlled by Satan and will turn you away from the Lord.

Think and choose:

1. The true Church will go to heaven and those who are left will then turn to God and accept Christ. FRAME 558

2. Many men do not really believe in Christ today but will believe the lying spirits before the Man of Sin appears. FRAME 562

3. There will be a great new religion in the world which will not have Christ as its head.   FRAME 564

556   You are right, none of these statements is true. Go to Frame 551.

557   Yes, we do, the Bible tells us that Christ will win the victory and Satan will be punished forever. Read Revelation 20.10 and look for the true statement.

558   No, those who are left will turn completely away from Christ. Read Frame 555 again.

559   Yes, this is true. Now go to Frame 555.

560   Now let us turn to Revelation 17 and read the whole chapter slowly and carefully. This chapter tells us about the great prostitute whom God is going to judge at the end of the Tribulation period.

A prostitute is a wicked woman who takes the place of a man's true wife to get money, 1 Corinthians 6.16. The true Church is like the Bride of Christ, Ephesians 5.25-27; Revelation 21.2,9; 22.17. So the great prostitute is a picture of the false church, and in Revelation 17 it is called Babylon the Great.

The great prostitute is a picture of all false religions:

1. She is immoral but very rich, v.4. Those who teach false religions are usually very rich because they make people pay money, but allow them to practice immorality.

2. Leaders of false religions have always hated God's people and killed many of them, Revelation 17.6; 18.24.

3. False religious leaders want to control the government and have often done so. So the great prostitute is seen sitting on the waters of the nations of the world and ruling over the kings of the world, Revelation 17.15,18.

Think and choose:

1. The great prostitute is called Babylon the Great and is a picture of the false church or of all false religion.

    FRAME 563

2. A rich religion must be true because God would not bless it if it was false.   FRAME 566

3. Many false religions attack God's people, try to run the government, and allow their members to be immoral.

    FRAME 569

561   Satan uses different methods to deceive the people of God and sometimes he is kind. But in the Tribulation he will attack God's people and persecute them and kill them. Read Revelation 12.13 and 13.4,7 again and look for a true statement.

562   This is very sad but it is true. Now look for another true statement.

563   True, but look for another true statement.

564   This is also true; if you understand both true statements go to Frame 560.

565   In Revelation 17 the great prostitute at first will have honour and glory. She will have control over the first beast, who will rule over the governments of the world, v.3. She will wear the clothing of a king or a queen, v.4.

But the ten horns of the first beast will turn against the great prostitute, v.16. These ten horns are pictures of ten kings. God will judge the great prostitute and put into the kings' hearts to kill her, v.17.

Other kings will cry and mourn for Babylon because they had

followed her false teaching, 18.9. Businessmen will also weep and mourn because they became rich with the help of their religion, 18.11. But God's people in heaven will be very glad because the great prostitute had killed so many of His servants, 19.1,2.

Think and choose:

1.   All the kings of the earth will mourn when Great Babylon is judged.   FRAME 567

2.   In the Great Tribulation false religion will at first control the governments or the countries of the world, but the first beast will turn against the great prostitute and destroy her.   FRAME 570

3.   Many businessmen get rich through false religion and they will be very sad when they lose this business.
                                                           FRAME 572

566   Not at all. Many sinful people can get rich in this world without God's blessing. False religions force the people to pay money so the priests and teachers become very rich while the people become poor. This is not a sign of God's blessing. Look again for a true statement.

567   No, the ten kings will turn against the great prostitute but other kings will mourn for her. Read Revelation 17.16 and 18.9 and Frame 565 again.

568   True, now find another true statement.

569   This is all true. But notice that the Lord commands us to come out of Babylon and all false religion, Revelation 18.4. True Christians should not mix with the false church or any false religion. Those who do will be very sorry. If you found both true statements go on to Frame 565.

570   Yes, it is important to remember this. Look for another true statement.

571   The great prostitute is a picture of the false church and all religion, and the first beast will turn against her and destroy her. Of course there are hundreds of different religions in the world today, but they are moving together. There are three large groups which call themselves Christian: the Roman Catholics, the Greek Orthodox, and the hundreds of Protestant denominations. Today Satan is trying to bring these different denominations and groups together: first the Protestants, then all those who are called Christians; then he will bring in other religions also.

Think and choose:

1. The great prostitute will be a picture of false religion but there are hundreds of false religions today.

    FRAME 568

2. The different religions of the world all hate each other and it would be impossible to bring them together.

    FRAME 573

3. Satan is now working to bring the different religious groups together and make them one.   FRAME 576

572   This is also true, go to Frame 571.

573   The different religions hate each other today, but Satan will be able to unite them because they all hate true Christians. Read Frame 571 again.

574   Every Protestant church believes something different from the others and you might wonder how Satan could ever get all Protestants together. This is what has happened:

1. The servants of Satan began to teach that the Bible is not all true, there are lies and mistakes in it. So people did not have anything they could really believe.

2. The Bible tells us what to believe, but if the Bible is not true we cannot be sure about anything. So Satan's servants teach that it does not matter what you believe as long as you try to help other people. Different churches believed these things and began to unite.

3. Then these people used a verse in the Bible, John 17.21, where the Lord prayed that His disciples may be one, just as He is

one with His Father. These men say this shows that God wants us to unite into one big church.

Think and choose:

1.   The Lord prayed that all Christians should be one and we should try to make His prayer come true.

FRAME 575

2.   What I do is more important than what I believe.

FRAME 578

3.   The servants of Satan teach that the Bible is not true, but they will use any verse in the Bible if it seems to prove what they want to say.   FRAME 580

575   God has made all true believers into one Body by giving us the Holy Spirit. The Lord did not pray that all churches should become one big organization or denomination. He certainly does not want us to join up with those who say the Bible is not true and that Christ is just a man. Look again for a true statement because this is wrong.

576   This is true, but is there another true statement? If you found both go on to Frame 574.

577   There are great differences among these religions but they agree on one thing, they hate Christ. They may join up with Protestants if the churches turn from Christ. Look for a better answer.

578   It is very important to believe the truth because those who believe false teaching will follow the Man of Sin, 2 Thessalonians 2.9-12. No one can be saved by doing good but anyone can be saved by believing in Christ, the Son of God. Try again.

579   For over 40 years Protestant churches have been talking about coming together and many denominations have joined each other to form bigger denominations. This is called the *ecumenical movement.* Still there are many true Christians who are not in favour of this coming together because it means that they must give up important doctrines. These true believers will go to heaven when the Lord comes and then all Protestants will be able to form one big denomination without believing in Christ at all.

Meanwhile the Roman Catholics and many Protestants have become quite friendly and in some cases are already working together. So Satan is getting them ready to make one big church including Roman Catholics, Protestants and Greek Orthodox.

There are many other religions which do not call themselves Christians, in fact, they have always hated Christians; for example, Moslems, Hindus, Buddhists. Today some leaders are already talking about a new religion which would include Moslems and Buddhists with those who call themselves Christians.

Think and choose:

1. Moslems believe in one God, Hindus believe in many gods and Buddhists do not even believe that God is a person. These religions will never agree to come together.   FRAME 577

2. Today we see great religions coming closer together and this is preparing the way for the false religion which is called the great prostitute or Babylon the Great.
                                                      FRAME 581

3. Today Roman Catholics are reading the Bible and this church will soon return to God and Christ, and millions will be saved.   FRAME 582

580   This is true. For example, they use John 17.21 to teach that there should be one great super Church in the world, even though many people in it would deny that Christ is One with the Father, which this same verse teaches very plainly. Think about these things, then go on to Frame 579.

581   This is true; go to Frame 583.

582   It is wonderful to see many Roman Catholics reading the Bible and all who trust in Christ will surely be saved. But the Bible does not give us any reason to believe that the Church of

Rome will ever turn to Christ and give up its false teaching. We should pray for people in the Roman Catholic Church that they may put their trust in Christ and hold firmly the truth they have, like the believers in Thyatira, Revelation 2.25. Look for a true statement.

583   We have seen that terrible things will happen in the last times. Wicked spirits will come in great numbers and will teach lies. Men will turn from the truth and form a great new religion without Christ. We can see the beginning of these things in the religions of today. But what about government? What does the Bible teach us about the governments of the future? Can we see any trends in the world now? Go right on to Lesson 12, the last lesson, Frame 584, and we will think about these questions.

12

THINGS BEGIN
TO HAPPEN

584　　The Lord Jesus said His disciples would know that salvation is near when these things begin to happen, Luke 21.28. We have seen what is taking place in the religions and the churches today and feel that the end must be near. We will now consider the governments of the world, the Gentile nations and the nation of Israel.

Some governments today say there is no God and others certainly do not love our Lord Jesus Christ. What should a Christian do? The Bible says he should obey the government of his country, Romans 13.1-7. But sometimes a government official may command you to worship an idol, or do some very wrong thing. In this case you should remember what Peter said in Acts 4.19 and 5.29, and be prepared to suffer for Christ.

Now go to Frame 586.

585　　Satan will be set free at the end of the Millennium and will find millions of men who will join together to fight against God. If you forgot about this, look up Revelation 20.7-9 and Frame 334.

This shows that many men will not love God even under the best conditions. They will soon follow a leader who will tell them to rebel against God. This proves that men must be born again, because we are all sinners by nature.

If you understand this Frame go on to Frame 592.

586   First think about the word *dispensation*. This word is used
for a period of time when God deals with men in a special
way. For example, we can speak of the dispensation of law
because God gave Israel His law. The dispensation of law lasted
from Moses to Christ, John 1.17.

The present time is the dispensation of grace, because now
God has revealed His grace through our Lord Jesus Christ. The
dispensation of grace is about the same period of time as the
Church Age; it started with Christ and lasts until the Rapture.

Think and choose:

1.   God has always loved men and has given His grace to all
     who believe; He will always do the same.   FRAME 588

2.   The word *dispensation* is used for a period of years, long
     or short, when God acts in a special way toward men,
     for example, the dispensation of law or the dispensation
     of grace.   FRAME 589

3.   Christians must keep God's law so the present time can
     be called the dispensation of law also.   FRAME 591

587   There have been other dispensations in the past and after
the Tribulation the Millennium will come, the last
dispensation. Why did God want to test men in different ways in
the different dispensations?

God has given men opportunity to do His will under different
conditions and men have always failed. Consider three
dispensations, *law, grace, tribulation.* Which one of these ended or
will end in:

1. Men nailing the Lord Jesus to the cross? _____

2. Men joining together to fight against God and His people?

_____

3. Men giving up faith in the Bible and in Christ?

_____

Write in the name of the dispensation which ended or will end
in this way. Turn to Frame 597 to see if you got the right answers.

588   It is true that God always loves men but there is a difference between law and grace. Read John 1.17 and Romans 11.6, then look again for the right answer.

589   True. Go to Frame 587.

590   So God tests men under different conditions in the different dispensations but men always fail. This shows that men need a Saviour and can never earn salvation by their own works.

Some people might say that God should give men another chance like they had in the Garden of Eden. They say men sin and commit crime because they do not have enough to eat. They start wars to get more land for the people....

God will answer this during the Millennium. There will be peace in the world and plenty of food, Frames 379 and 395. Christ will punish at once anyone who breaks the law. People will know what sin is and that they should not commit sin. What will be the results of all this? Will men love God?

What will happen at the end of the Millennium? _____
_____

How does this prove that men need a Saviour? _____
_____

Write out your answers to these two questions in your own words, then turn to Frame 585 to see if you got them right.

591   All believers are saved by grace and we are not under the law but under grace, Romans 6.14. Many people do not understand the grace of God nor believe that Christ has paid fully for our sins. They think they have to keep the law in order to be saved. This is a terrible mistake. If you are trusting in your own works please turn to Christ right now and accept Him as your Saviour. Go back to Frame 586 and find the true statement.

592   We have learned from the Old Testament prophets that the Lord would come in two different ways; they said He would come and be rejected by men and He would come in power and glory. Now we understand that there is a long period of time between the first and second coming of Christ. There is also a gap after the fourth empire and before the end time. Daniel predicted that the little horn would fight against God's people, until Christ comes to deliver them, Daniel 7.19-22. This little horn is a king of the fourth empire, Rome. He will be in the world during the Tribulation period until the Lord comes. So the fourth empire will become very strong again at the end.

Think and choose:

1. The time of the Gentiles will continue until the Lord Jesus comes again and the little horn will fight against the Jews until God judges him.   FRAME 594

2. The Roman Empire fell about 1,400 years ago and Italy is not one of the greatest nations today. So we cannot expect the little horn to rule in the last days.
                                                      FRAME 596

3. There has been a gap between the first and second comings of Christ and also between the times when the fourth beast had great power in the past and will have again in the future.   FRAME 599

593   The Roman Empire was the greatest of the four empires which Daniel prophesied would rule in the world. The Roman Empire covered most of Europe and the lands around the Mediterranean Sea. About 500 years after the time of Christ the Roman Empire lost its power and came to an end. Since then no government has been able to control all the countries of Europe.

Today ten countries of Europe have partly united, but no one country controls all the others. Remember that the fourth beast had **ten** horns which are pictures of ten kings, Daniel 7.23,24. The little horn will defeat three of these kings and become the greatest of the ten. This will take place during the Tribulation and before the Lord comes in power and glory.

Think and choose:

1. Ten nations in the old Roman Empire have partly united and this also shows that Christ may soon come again.   FRAME 595

2. Russia is the greatest single nation in Europe today and it will soon gain control over the other countries.
                                                    FRAME 598

3. The little horn came out of the fourth beast and a great leader of Europe will appear during the Tribulation. He will bring the nations of Europe together and rule over them.   FRAME 601

594   True, so we can be sure that the little horn will be alive and have great power at the end of the times of the Gentiles. Now find another true statement.

595   Very good; look for another statement.

596   The first part of your answer is true but the Bible plainly shows that the little horn comes out of the Roman Empire and that he will have power to fight against Israel until the Lord comes. This does not mean that Italy will become a great country and rule over all Europe. Italy does not appear to be a great nation today, but things can change very rapidly. Look again for a true statement.

597   Israel nailed Christ to the cross at the end of the dispensation of law. Men will join together to fight against God at the end of the Tribulation period. Most people called Christians will give up their faith in the Bible and in Christ at the end of the dispensation of grace or the Church Age. Their leaders are telling them that the Bible is not true and that Christ is not the only Son of God.

Every dispensation ends in the failure of men but this need not be true of each man's life. Let us walk with the Lord, study the Bible, and serve Him. We will be able to say the same words as Paul in 2 Timothy 4.7.

If you understand these answers go to Frame 590.

598   The Bible does not say that Russia will rule over Europe, but no doubt it will be an enemy of Israel in the last days. Look for a true statement.

599   Good; if you understand the two true statements go to Frame 593.

600   The Bible speaks of other great Gentile nations at the end of the age. **Gog** will lead the people of Magog, Meshech and Tubal against the land of Israel, with other nations also, Ezekiel 38.1-6. In Revelation 20.8 Magog stands for all nations which will again go up to destroy Israel and will be destroyed by God.

In Daniel 11.40 we also read about the king of the north in the last times. We can read about the Assyrian king who also will attack God's people, Micah 5.5. Assyria lies to the north of Israel, so the Assyrian may be the same as the king of the north.

Daniel 11.40 also speaks of the king of the south which means the king of Egypt. In Revelation 16.12 we read about the kings of the east coming across the Euphrates River. We cannot always tell the modern name of these countries but we can see that God still controls all nations and He could tell long ago what will happen soon.

Think and choose:

1.   Gog, king of Magog, will lead Gentile armies against Israel in the Tribulation period, then again after the Millennium.   FRAME 602

2.   The Bible tells us a little about the nations of the world in the end time. Some of them will attack God's people until the Lord comes.   FRAME 604

3.   The king of the north may control Assyria which will be north of Israel; the king of the south will rule over Egypt which is south of Israel.   FRAME 607

601   This is true; if you understand both true statements go to Frame 600.

602   No, the leaders of Gentile armies will be killed at the end of the Tribulation, Revelation 19.19. After the Millennium the nations will again go up against Jerusalem, and the leader may take the same name Gog, but it will not be the same man who died long before. Look for a true statement.

603   What about Israel? Does the Bible say anything about Israel which is beginning to happen today? Yes, it does. The Bible teaches us that the nation of Israel will be in their land during the Tribulation.

1. The beast will make a **covenant** with Israel for seven years, Daniel 9.27. This shows that Israel will be known as a nation.

2. Israel will be living in the land of Judea, Matthew 24.16 (only those who are there could run away from it).

3. The temple of Israel will be in Jerusalem and at first the beast will allow the people to offer sacrifices there. Later he will stop them by defiling the altar with the Abomination of Desolation, Matthew 24.15.

Think and choose:

1.   Israel will be a nation in its own land with the temple in Jerusalem before the Great Tribulation begins.

FRAME 609

2.   The Jews could build their temple any place in the world and God would accept their worship. FRAME 611

604   This is true, but look again for another true answer.

605   This is true. Now look for another true statement.

606   This is also true. It is exciting to see these events happening and to know that the Lord will soon come and change things in this world. We ought to live holy and dedicated lives as we wait for that great Day, 2 Peter 3.11,12.

If you understand both true statements, go to Frame 612.

607   This is also true. Go to Frame 603.

608   The armies of Rome destroyed Jerusalem and the temple about 70 years after Christ was born. The people of Israel were forced to run away to other lands, but still God looked after them for hundreds of years. They did not have a land of their own to live in but had to live with other nations.

In 1948 Israel regained most of their old land and became a nation once more. However they had only part of the holy city of Jerusalem and could not build the temple again on the same place where it was before. In 1967 Israel gained control over the rest of the land and all the city of Jerusalem.

Think about the following statements and choose one or two which are true.

1.   For 1,878 years the Jewish people lived in many countries, but Israel did not exist as a nation or possess their own land.   FRAME 605

2.   Today Israel is a nation and in its old land, but it still does not have a temple.   FRAME 606

3.   The Rapture cannot occur until the Jews have built their temple in Jerusalem.   FRAME 610

609   True, go to Frame 608.

610   Wrong. The Lord could come and the Rapture could occur at any time. The Scripture says the Jews will have their temple in Jerusalem before the middle of the Tribulation period, but they could start building soon after the Rapture. Look again.

611   God chose Jerusalem as the place where Israel should worship Him and we can be sure that Israel will build the new temple right there. Look for the true statement.

612   Let us now think about what will happen in the first half of Daniel's 70th week, the first three and a half years of the Tribulation. We will see that conditions in the world today are pointing to the same things.

1. The Lord Jesus described the beginning of Pain in Matthew 24.5-8. Read these verses and also read Frame 186.

2. The beast will make a covenant with Israel, Daniel 9.27, Frame 506, and allow them to build the temple in Jerusalem.

3. The Lord will open the seals of the book and trouble will start on the earth. Read Revelation 6.1-17 and Frame 476.

These things will happen during the beginning of Pain in the first half of the Tribulation. Which of them do we see happening in the world today more often or worse than before? Write **Yes** or **No** or **Don't know** after each event.

TODAY

1. Wars, Matthew 24.6; Revelation 6.3,4 ....

2. Nations conquered, Revelation 6.2 ....

3. The beast makes a covenant with Israel,
     Daniel 9.27 ....

4. The temple built in Jerusalem ....

5. Great hunger in many countries, Matthew
     24.7; Revelation 6.5,6 ....

6. Earthquakes, Matthew 24.7 ....

7. False prophets and false christs, Matthew 24.5,11 ....

8. One fourth of all people will die, Revelation 6.8. ....

9. Sun black, moon red, and stars fall,
     Revelation 6.12,13 ....

10. Fear, Revelation 6.15-17 ....

Write in your answers, *yes* or *no* or *don't know*. Then turn to Frame 613 to see if you are right.

613 1. Yes. There always have been wars in the world, but they are becoming more frequent and more terrible. There were 93 wars in the last 150 years, in which 29 million people were killed.

2. No. Today nations are dividing up and there are far more nations than there were a few years ago. In the Tribulation one man will win control over many nations.

3. No. This will not take place until after the Rapture.

4. No. The temple can be built only on one spot and today a Moslem mosque is there.

5. No. Millions of people do not have enough food to eat but not many really starve to death.

6. Yes. Earthquakes are happening more often than before.

7. Yes, there are many false prophets today and some claim to be the Messiah or Christ.

8. No. People live longer today and the population of the world is greater than ever.

9. No. These signs will be seen during the Tribulation period.

10. Yes. Men everywhere are afraid of what may happen next; even government leaders are not sure of the future.

Go on to Frame 614.

614   Many things are happening today which will become far worse during the Tribulation. Surely the Lord will soon come, perhaps very soon. We do not and cannot know the date, but we should be ready. These things are beginning to happen.... We should stand up and raise our heads because our Saviour must be near.

ANSWERS TO QUESTIONS ON CHART 9

1. Babylon, Rome.

2. The time of the Gentiles began when the king of Babylon captured and destroyed Jerusalem. It will continue until the Lord comes back as King.

3. The Church Age started when the Holy Spirit came down on the day of Pentecost and it will continue until the Rapture.

4. The last four periods of the Church Age will continue until the Rapture.

5. The Rapture.

6. All believers must stand before the Lord at the Judgment Seat of Christ.

7. The Tribulation period will start.

8. The seals will come first and the bowls last. There are seven of each of these.

9. The Wedding Feast of Christ will take place after the Judgment Seat.

10. The two beasts will be thrown into the lake of fire when the Lord comes and Satan will be bound for 1,000 years.

11. The Lord will rule as King on this earth for 1,000 years.

12. Satan will be finally thrown into the lake of fire.

13. People who are judged at the Great White Throne will go to the lake of fire.

14. The New Heaven and Earth will last for ever and ever.

If you understand Chart 9 and these questions and answers go on to Frame 534, Lesson 11.

Word List and Index

Abomination of Desolation A wicked king made God's temple at Jerusalem unclean or desolate. This is called the Abomination of Desolation. This king is a picture of the beast in the Tribulation period. Frames 168, 196, 470, 506

Angels Frames 26, 208

Antichrist A great religious leader during the Tribulation period. Frames 412, 462

  Antichrists False messiahs. Many enemies of Christ are called antichrists. Some claim to be Christ or a messiah and especially in the last days there will be many who will do this. Frame 208

Antiochus Epiphanes was a king of part of the Greek empire. He attacked Israel and made God's temple unclean with the Abomination of Desolation. Frames 161, 168

Apostasy Many people turn away from Christ and the Scripture and some do not want to be called "Christians" any more. After the Rapture the churches will turn away from the Lord Jesus Christ and follow the Antichrist. This is called the Apostasy. Frames 429, 555

Archangel The chief angel. Frame 51

Asleep in Jesus A believer who dies is asleep in Jesus. This means his body is resting until the resurrection; his spirit is very happy with the Lord. Frame 42

Babylon was the first great kingdom in Daniel's dream. Nebuchadnezzar, king of Babylon, defeated the Jews and took many of them as prisoners. Frames 139, 169, 172

Babylon the Great is a name for the great prostitute in the book of Revelation. Frames 560, 565

Beast The first beast will be the great leader of the Tribulation period who will be worshipped by men. Frames 318, 434, 438, 442, 458, 462

Beginning of Pain The first half of the Tribulation period, described in Matthew 24.5-8 and Revelation 6. Frames 186, 493, 612

Body of Christ A name for the true Church; Christ is the Head of the Body.   Frames 238, 241

Bowls of Wrath Seven bowls of God's wrath will be poured out in the second half of the Tribulation.   Frames 488, 489

Bride of Christ Christ loves the Church as a man loves his wife.   Frame 303

Charts The time charts show the main events in God's plan for men, from the time of the Gentiles to the new Heaven and the new Earth   Frames 34, 96, 127, 178, 237, 302, 359, 469, 533

Christ   Frames 117, 132, 147, 172

Christ, the Head of the Church   Frame 252

Christ will come with power and glory   Frames 208, 224, 313

Christ the King   Frame 379

Christ the Judge   Frame 341

Christs, False   Frame 412

Church The Church is the Body of Christ.   Frame 238

The History of the Church   Frames 260, 300

The Rapture of the Church   Look up the word Rapture.

Teaching about the Church is in the New Testament Frame 375

Churches of Asia The Lord sent messages to seven churches in the province of Asia.   Frame 257, Lesson 6

Conflict of the Ages Started when Satan first sinned against God and will continue until the time he is thrown into the lake of fire after the Millennium.   Frame 551

Daniel the Prophet   Frames 97, 100, 104, 128

Daniel's Dream   Frame 132, 135, 139

Daniel's Vision   Frame 153

Date setting Many people have tried to say that Christ will come on some special date but the Bible tells us that no one knows the date except the Father.   Frame 179

David the King   Frame 379

Dispensations are ages or periods of time when God deals with men in a special way.   Frames 586, 587

Earth God will destroy this earth with fire and create a new one.   Frames 345, 407

Ecumenical Movement This is the plan to bring Protestant Churches together and make one big super Church. This will then join with Roman Catholics and Greek Orthodox Churches.   Frames 571, 574, 579

Ephesus The first of the seven churches, is a picture of the early Church in the time of the apostles.   Frame 263

Eternity is time which has no end.   Frame 355

Europe The Roman Empire controlled most of Europe and today ten countries of Europe are coming together again. Frame 593

False Prophet The False Prophet will be the head of the religions which will unite in the Tribulation period. He will put a mark on people and make them worship the beast.   Frames 417, 458, 462

First Beast The first beast of Revelation 13 will be the great leader of the Tribulation period who will be worshipped by men.   Frames 318, 434, 438, 442, 458, 462

Gentiles All people who are not Jews are called Gentiles. The time of the Gentiles started when the king of Babylon destroyed Jerusalem and will continue until the Lord comes back to rule as King of Israel and King of the world.
Frame 172

The Judgment of Living Gentiles will take place when the Lord comes with power and glory.   Frame 233

God is full of grace   Frame 292

God knows the future   Frame 46

Gog will be the ruler of a great nation called Magog   Frame 600

Government   Frame 439

Great White Throne The Lord Jesus Christ will judge all wicked and unsaved men at the end of the Millennium.
Frames 337, 341

Greece The third kingdom in Daniel's dream.   Frame 157

Heaven is where God is.   Frames 348, 353, 391, 395

New Heaven Heaven will pass away and God will create a New Heaven after the Millennium.   Frames 345, 407

Hell is the place where unsaved people go when they die; sometimes this word means the lake of fire.   Frames 351, 353

Holy Spirit   Frames 32, 431

Media The second kingdom of Daniel's dream. Frame 153

Millennium A thousand years when the Lord Jesus Christ will rule as King over the world. See Lesson 8. Frames 323, 327, 590

Nebuchadnezzar The first king of Babylon. Frames 112, 135

Pentecost The 50th day after the Lord Jesus was crucified, when the Holy Spirit came down and the Church was formed. Frame 241

Pergamum The third church of Revelation 2, a picture of the third part of the Church Age. Frame 273

Persia Joined with Media to form the second kingdom of Daniel's dream. Frame 153

Philadelphia The sixth church of Revelation 2 and 3, a picture of the sixth part of the Church Age. Frames 292, 296

Promises of the first coming of Christ. Frames 360, 366

  Promises of the second coming of Christ. Frames 7, 15, 26, 30, 366, 370

  Promise to send the Holy Spirit. Frame 32

Prophets of the Old Testament can be trusted. Frame 121

  Prophets, False   Frames 192, 208, 318

Prostitute, Great A picture of the False Church of the future, and of all false religions. Frames 560, 565

Protestant Churches Frame 288

Rapture The Lord Jesus Christ will come to the clouds and His Church will be caught up to meet Him. Frames 61, 67, 68, 74, 375

  Rapture - order of events   Frames 46, 55

  Rapture - time of Frame 80

  Rapture - different from the time when Christ comes with power and glory. Frame 224

Religions Frame 399

Remnant A small number of true believers who live in a larger group of people who say they believe but are lying. Frames 283, 288, 292

Resurrection The Lord Jesus Christ rose from death. Frame 42 He will raise the bodies of God's people. Frames 55, 327

He will raise all wicked men.   Frame 337

Rewards The Lord Jesus Christ will give rewards at the Judgment Seat of Christ to those who serve Him.   Frames 81, 84

Rome is the fourth great kingdom of Daniel's dream.   Frames 169, 278, 592, 593

Sardis is the fifth church of the Church Age.   Frame 288

Satan   Frames 323, 334, 442, 551

Scriptures The Scriptures helped Daniel.   Frame 128
    We can trust the Bible.   Frame 121

Second Beast of Revelation 13, is also called the False Prophet and the Antichrist; he will be the great religious leader during the Tribulation period.   Frames 446, 451, 458, 462

Second Coming of the Son of Man.   Frames 208, 313
    Reasons for the Second Coming   Frames 7, 13
    Two parts of the Second Coming   Frames 370, 592

Seven Seals The Lord Jesus will open these seals and trouble will start to come to men on earth.   Frames 476, 612

Seventy Weeks The angel told Daniel that God planned seventy weeks or 490 years for Israel.   Frames 500, 504

Signs are events which happen in the world to show believers that God's time is coming close.   Frame 211

Sleep in the Bible sometimes means the death of a believer. Frame 42

Smyrna was the second church of the Church Age. Frame 268

Spirits Satan can send evil spirits to teach lies to men who are willing to listen.   Frames 489, 543, 548

Sun, Moon and Stars There will be signs in space before the Lord comes.   Frame 208

Temple of God The Jews will build a temple in Jerusalem during the Tribulation and Christ will build another in the Millennium.   Frames 220, 381, 603, 608

Thyatira The fourth church of the Church Age. Frames 278, 283

Tribulation A period of great trouble which will start after the Rapture. Frames 192, 196, 204, 308, 470, 475, 511
    Length of the Tribulation.   Frames 493, 497, 504
    The Tribulation not for the Church.   Frames 514, 518, 523

The first half of the Tribulation.   Frame 612

Trinity   Frame 463

Trumpet of God   Frames 51, 74

Trumpets Seven angels will blow their trumpets during the Great Tribulation.   Frame 479, 484, 485

Union of Europe   Frame 593

Union of Religions   Frames 571, 574, 579

Wedding Feast   A time of great joy for the Lord Jesus and His Church after the judgment seat of Christ.   Frame 303

Wicked One   Another name for the Man of Sin.   Frames 421, 425

TEST YOURSELF

By now you know the most important events which are explained in this Primer on Prophecy. You should be able to get most of these answers without looking at page 190. If you forget something, you can look at your Bible or any Frame in this program. Write out your answers on a separate piece of paper, then look at page 192 just to make sure.

1. Who said that Daniel was a prophet?
2. How many wild animals did Daniel see in his dream?
3. What are these animals a picture of?
4. What is the name of the kingdom which had great power when Daniel was living?
5. What is the name of the kingdom which had great power when Christ was living?
6. When did the time of the Gentiles begin? When will it end?
7. When did the Church Age begin?
8. How long will it continue?
9. How many periods are there in the Church Age?
10. Which was the first church in Revelation 2 and 3?
11. Name at least two other churches in Revelation 2 and 3.
12. How many of the seven periods of the Church Age will continue until Christ comes?
13. Which of these do we see in the world today?
14. Israel is a nation today (True/False). Choose your answer.
15. Israel has its own temple today (True/False, choose).
16. How long has Israel been in its land?
17. How many countries in Europe are united?
18. Why is this important?
19. Religions of the world are coming together today. Why is this important?
20. What is the first part of the second coming called?
21. Who knows when it will take place?

22. Who will go to be with the Lord at that time?
23. Where will they meet Christ?
24. How long will they be with Him?
25. What kind of "Christians" will be left behind when the Lord comes?
26. Which believers will stand before the Judgment Seat of Christ?
27. Who will receive crowns and rewards?
28. Daniel prophesied about 70 weeks. Each week is equal to .... years (fill in the number of years).
29. When was the 69th week over?
30. When will the 70th week be over?
31. What do we call the first part of the 70th week? .... What do we call the second part? ....
32. How many seals will be opened in the first part of the 70th week?
33. When will the trumpets be sounded?
34. What will the bowls contain?
35. Name two great leaders in the future.
36. Which one will make an agreement with the Jews?
37. How long will he keep this agreement?
38. What is the Abomination of Desolation?
39. What should the Jews do when they see the Abomination of Desolation?
40. What will men do to this king?
41. Who will try to put a mark on all men?
42. What is the great prostitute a picture of?
43. What will happen to her?
44. How long will people worship men and persecute true believers?
45. What will take place in heaven after the Judgment Seat of Christ?
46. How will people know when Christ comes back?
47. What will Christ do with the two men who will persecute His people?
48. What will He do to men who follow these leaders?
49. What will He do to other people?

50. What will He do to Satan?
51. How long will Christ rule as King in this world?
52. What will it be like when Christ is King? (Answer yes or no.)

    Will there be wars on the world?   ....

    Will there be enough food?   ....

    Will there be any false religion?   ....

    Will there be a place to worship God?   ....

53. After the Millennium what will happen to Satan?
54. What will he do then?
55. Where will God put Satan?
56. Who must stand before Christ when He sits on the Great White Throne?
57. Where will He send them?
58. What will happen to heaven and earth?
59. How long will the new heaven and earth last?
60. How long is Eternity?

CHECK YOUR ANSWERS

1. The Lord Jesus Christ, Frame 97.
2. Four, Frame 132.
3. Four kingdoms, Frame 139.
4. Babylon, Frame 139.
5. Rome, Frame 169.
6. The time of the Gentiles started when God gave Israel into the power of Babylon and it will last until Christ returns, Frame 172.
7. When the Holy Spirit came down on the day of Pentecost, Frame 241.
8. Until Christ comes for His Church, Frame 241.
9. Seven, Frame 260.
10. Ephesus; Laodicea, Frames 263, 299.
11. Smyrna, Pergamum, Thyatira, Sardis, Philadelphia.
12. Four, Frame 300.
13. All four, Frame 302.
14. True, Frame 603.
15. False, Frame 603.
16. Since 1948, Frame 608.
17. Ten, Frame 593.
18. Long ago Rome controlled most of Europe and a king of the fourth empire will have great power before the Lord comes in His glory. A wild animal with ten horns is a picture of this king, Frame 593.
19. It shows that we are getting near the end of this age, Frame 579.
20. The Rapture, Frame 224.
21. The Father, Frame 179.
22. All believers, Frame 523.
23. In the clouds, Frame 61.
24. Forever, Frame 63.
25. Only those who are not real believers, who only say they are Christ's, Frame 514.

26. All, Frame 84.
27. Only those who have served the Lord well and faithfully, Frame 230.
28. Seven years, Frame 500.
29. When the Messiah was cut off, Frame 504.
30. When Christ comes to rule the world, Frame 500.
31. The beginning of Pain; the Great Tribulation, Frame 493.
32. Seven, Frame 476, 479.
33. In the second part of the 70th week, Frame 479.
34. God's wrath, Frame 488.
35. The beast and the False Prophet, Frame 462.
36. The Beast, Frame 511.
37. Three and one half years, Frame 506.
38. A king will stop the Jews from worshipping God by setting up an idol in the temple, Frame 196.
39. Run away as soon as possible, Frame 196.
40. Worship him, Frame 451.
41. The second beast, Frame 454.
42. False Religion, Frame 560.
43. God will judge her and the ten kings will turn against her, Frame 565.
44. Until Christ comes, Frames 438, 442, 458.
45. The Wedding Feast of the Lamb, Frame 303.
46. He will come with power and glory and everyone will see Him, Frame 208.
47. Throw them into the lake of fire, Frame 458.
48. He will destroy them, Frame 313.
49. Judge them. Believers will enter His Kingdom, others will go to the lake of fire, Frame 233.
50. Satan will be thrown into a hole for a thousand years, Frame 323.
51. A thousand years, Frame 327.
52. No wars; lots of food; no false religion; yes, Jerusalem. Frames 381, 395, 399.
53. He will be loosed, Frame 334.
54. He will gather men to fight against God, Frame 334.

55. In the lake of fire, Frame 334.
56. All wicked men, Frame 337.
57. To the lake of fire, Frame 337.
58. They will be burned up, Frame 345.
59. For ever, Frame 345.
60. It has no end, it will last as long as God exists, Frame 355.

How many answers did you get right? If you got 50 right answers before you looked up the Answer Page, you did very well. This shows that you know the most important ideas of Prophecy.

You will remember these ideas better if you teach them to someone else. You will also

— *help him to understand God's plans;*
— *give him a wonderful hope that the Lord Jesus Christ will come again;*
— *show him why we should live according to God's will.*